CIRCE

A young woman's memories of tuberculosis treatment
in the 1950s

By Isabel Gillard

With a medical history of TB by Sir John Crofton

Illustrations by Jayne Watson

Unbound Press
Circe's Island
An Unbound Press Book: ISBN 978-0-9558360-5-3

Originally published in Great Britain
by Unbound Press 2010

Unbound Press Books are published by
Unbound Press
Apartment 3/1, 54 Hughenden Lane, Glasgow, G12 9XJ
www.unboundpress.com

Dedicated to the memory of

Sir Robert Philip (1857-1939)

and

Sir John Crofton (1912-2009)

who outmanoeuvred the enchantress

'Is it to rescue thy comrades that thou art come?

Circe has changed them.'

(Homer's Odyssey)

ABOUT THE AUTHOR: Isabel Gillard is an expatriate Scot, born in Edinburgh and resident in the Midlands since her marriage in 1958. She has earned her living as a teacher of literature with a strong creative writing component and has herself won a number of small awards, mainly for poetry, short stories and articles. Her other literary hats include occasional broadcasts and a spell as poetry-writing tutor at Keele University. She has compiled and edited numerous anthologies of poetry and a quarterly prose and poetry magazine, *Distaff,* for West Midlands Arts. She has also written one successful play, a *son et lumiere* based on village history, and two novels, one of which, *Yewberry Fall*, won a Book of the Year award judged by Three Counties Radio.

After a fairly busy life, she and her husband enjoy frequent contact with their two daughters and five grandchildren and live in a 'visited' cottage in the Midlands keeping the peace between their two cats.

ABOUT THE ILLUSTRATOR: Jayne Watson's background is in graphics and design for print. She has spent the last 15 years working in the greeting card industry and has recently started her own company, The Hare & Moon Press.

CONTENTS

ACKNOWLEDGEMENTS

I would like to record my heartfelt thanks to Sir John Crofton – of legendary fame in the annals of TB treatment and cure – for his valuable support, ready listening ear and generous involvement in this project; Dr Andrew Fairfax, BSc, MB BS, MRCP, for being a willing reader and helping to keep the record straight, and medical friends Charles De Boer, retired Consultant, Dr M. Mulligan, General Practitioner, and Dr Hugh Platt, OBE, TD, BSc.,MD, FRCPath., FRCOpth., FRCP, for their interest, advice and support.

In addition I am hugely grateful to my sister, Louise Strahan, for her unstinting support in times of crisis and to my husband, Peter Gillard, who stretched time sufficiently for me to write the book.

Copyright permissions:

By permission of archive section of Newcastle-under-Lyme Library: quotes from *At Loggerheads with the Enemy*, compiled by Paul Bemrose (Newcastle-under-Lyme Borough Council, 1981)

By permission of Oxford University Press and Professor Linda Bryder: use of material from *Below the Magic Mountain, A Social History of Tuberculosis in 20th Century Britain* by Linda Bryder (Oxford University Press, 1988)

A percentage of the author's royalties on sales will go to the World Health Organization to further the control of TB and leprosy throughout the world

PREFACE

In 1950, when I was still a student at Edinburgh University, I was found to be suffering from TB and hospitalised in the sanatorium known as the Royal Victoria Hospital for Tuberculosis. There I spent a substantial part of the sixteen months that I was out of circulation. I was in serious danger; relatively few people survived and none was considered cured. TB was at that time incurable. However, the medication and surgical procedures came and went, I survived the cold 'cure' and I picked up my life again.

In the course of exploring and reliving this experience I became aware of being part of an enormous success story. This lethal disease, that had held sway over humankind since prehistory, was on the verge of being conquered, thanks in part to the work of two eminent Edinburgh medical men. Sir Robert Philip was the Edinburgh doctor who, at the start of the twentieth century, set up the Edinburgh System which brought some control over the disease. Sir John Crofton, like Sir Robert Philip, was Professor of Tuberculosis at Edinburgh University and was knighted for getting the runaway mortality figures under control in the 1950s. In the UK the TB mortality rate is now down from 306:100,000 to fewer than 1:100,000.

Sir John heard of my book and asked to meet me. I was glad of the chance to return to Edinburgh for a couple of days and spent an animated afternoon with him and his wife. He offered me an introduction to my book, *Circe's Island,* and an appendix giving the details of his war and post-war experience in the medical field, the world situation at the present time, the complication of HIV, and what is being done to contain TB on a global scale.

He read and enjoyed my account of sanatorium life in 1950 and described it as a valuable document in recording the transition from the traditional, classic treatment for the disease to the successful treatment of today. I was staggered by the generosity of someone of his eminence, aged 97, doing this for a complete stranger and feel that the publication of *Circe's Island* is a fitting tribute to this unique man. I am indebted to *Unbound Press* for bringing this about.

Isabel Gillard

INTRODUCTION

Tuberculosis (formerly sometimes called *phthisis* from the Greek for *consumption*: in English, now more often and colloquially called TB) is probably mankind's most ancient disease. Indeed recent analysis of the history of the DNA of the Tuberculosis Bacillus suggests that in prehistory it mutated from a common soil bacillus to cause illness in mankind. This may have occurred as early as the hominid ancestors of *Homo sapiens* walked the earth.

It used to be thought that the soil bacillus had first mutated to cause disease in cows when these had been domesticated in the Neolithic farming revolution. The bovine bacillus might then have mutated to cause human disease. But the recent historical DNA evidence suggests that it was actually the other way round, from man to cows.

It is generally agreed that Homo sapiens originated in Africa. Evidence of bone tuberculosis has been found in Nubian mummies as early as 3,000 BC. Suggestive disease descriptions also appeared early in China. In Europe clinical symptoms of TB were recorded by the Greek Hippocrates in the 5th century BC.

The Romans probably brought the disease to the UK. Bone TB is found quite frequently in subsequent burials. Only one or two isolated TB burials from pre-Roman times have been found in Southwest England, possibly a residuum of visits by Phoenician tin traders.

In the Americas one or two cases have been claimed in frozen mummies high up in the Andes and later in pre-Columbian cities in Meso-America but TB assumed epidemic proportions when, together with smallpox, measles and other European infections, it wiped out vast numbers of Native Americans after 1492.

According to the Penguin Economic History of Europe, although plague and cholera produced recurrent brief high mortality in mediaeval times, the great *continuous* killer of many bread-earners and their families was TB.

In England, following the Industrial Revolution, with the great overcrowding and poverty in the new industrial cities, by the mid-nineteenth century one in seven of all adult deaths was due to TB. But later in the century, as imported food improved the nutrition of the labouring classes and overcrowding decreased, mortality gradually diminished, though remaining very high until the mid 20th century. Incidence increased briefly in England when the sanatoria were emptied in 1939 so as to accommodate expected air raid casualties.

There was considerable medical argument during the early 19th century as to whether TB was a congenital disease, as it often affected multiple family members, or, following Pasteur's discovery of bacteria, whether it was an infection. This was resolved in 1882 when Koch in Germany proved conclusively that the tubercle bacillus, Mycobacterium tuberculosis, was the cause.*

SIR ROBERT PHILIP

Around 1880 Sir Robert Philip of Edinburgh travelled, as many did at that time, to Vienna to undertake postgraduate study in one of its famous laboratories. While he was there Koch's discovery was announced. The Vienna laboratory immediately switched its interest to the new bacillus.

Sir Robert returned to Edinburgh full of enthusiasm. If TB was an infectious disease it might be prevented. One of Philip's seniors advised him on his return to Edinburgh, 'Philip, phthisis is played out. Take up something else.' But Philip was a strong character. He started working in a charity clinic for the poor where he saw vast numbers of TB among the sick. So he devised his 'Edinburgh System'.

Infectious patients with far advanced disease were sent to the newly built City Hospital for Infectious Diseases. Philip raised money for a Trust to found the Royal Victoria Hospital. The primary contacts of the advanced cases were called up by nurses from his TB dispensary. If these patients had early mild disease which might respond to strict bed rest and good food, adults would be admitted to the Royal Victoria Hospital, children to a children's hospital. He also started a farm where recovering patients could gradually increase their physical labour along the lines used in the sanatoria.

Philip's System had the great advantage over the increasingly used Sanatorium System in that most of its components were readily accessible for patients and relatives in the city whereas sanatoria were often in the depths of the country.

As so often with pioneers, it was not until twenty years later, at St Mary's Hospital in London, that Philip's Edinburgh System was taken up. With London's support to pressurise the government, legislation in 1911 handed over responsibility for TB to local authorities, using the Edinburgh System. Philip received a knighthood. In 1919 the Trust which he had so successfully initiated, founded a Professorship at Edinburgh University and provided him with professorial beds at a semi-country house at Southfield which I inherited in due course.

Besides his professional salary which was quite small, Philip also had an extensive private practice. I gathered from those who worked for him that if some new treatment for TB appeared in the media Philip always claimed, often incorrectly, that he was already using it in Edinburgh. His private practice was frequented by middle and upper class patients and in those days there was a distinct view that the sick poor were a slightly different species. 'They don't feel pain like us,' was never definitely expressed but was often implied by action. For instance the wonderful Sister who later ran the Royal Victoria TB Dispensary founded by Philip, told me that when she took over there was a little room where stretcher patients were put before seeing the doctor. In the same room were glass cases illustrating TB pathology which Philip used for teaching. One of these glass cases contained a child split vertically down the middle to demonstrate the TB pathology in his innards. Her first priority was to provide a curtain to hide this from terrified stretcher patients.

In *Circe's Island* there is a Dr E whose attitude to patients and way of addressing them is explained by the need to ensure patients observed the requirements of strict bed rest. I had already heard from other patients, referred from Edinburgh to my pneumothorax clinic at the Brompton Hospital in London, that Dr E would say, 'You're like rosy apples rotten at the core,' to the poor girls who were afflicted by an illness which would kill at least half of them. Another patient told a colleague that one day, with no warning, an ambulance had picked her up at the Royal Victoria Hospital and brought her to the City Hospital. When Dr E next came round the City Hospital ward she dared to ask him why she had been moved. He replied, 'You will see, dear, that the Royal Victoria Hospital has no autopsy room.'

On my appointment as Professor of Tuberculosis at Edinburgh University it had been agreed that when Dr E retired in three years time, my team would become responsible for all clinical TB control. I tried to pass on to Dr E some of the advances in chemotherapy which were emerging from the Medical Research Council and our own research – but in vain. It was good for all concerned when Dr E retired a year early.

When Philip died in 1939 in his eighties, while still the Professor, the University decided to appoint Professor Cameron as the acting Professor during the 1939-45 war after which he would soon be due to retire. Thereafter the University would appoint a younger man, who turned out to be me. Cameron had immense knowledge and experience of TB and carried out most technical procedures personally with great technical skill. He had the reputation of being a difficult master and teacher of his staff but I was delighted to read how much trouble he took to ensure that Bella Strahan returned to her University studies after carefully considering her medical needs.

Professor Sir John Crofton

*[Reference: The history of tuberculosis – from earliest times to the development of drugs. Roberts C, Buikstra J. In *Clinical Tuberculosis* 4th ed. Davies P.D.O, Barnes P.F, Gordon S.B eds. Hodder, Arnold 2008]

CHAPTER 1
A Rude Awakening

I am awake in the middle of the night and I am cold. Not ordinary cold. Not shivery. I am frozen to the marrow. I do not know where I am and search for the sensations that will tell me.

There are draughts funnelling down both sides of my body under tight-wrapped sheets, smooth and cold as glass. I tug at the tucked edges, but they will not be moved. My knees are raised, making a tent further down the bed. They are stiff and aching. I decide to lie flat; that should stop the frigid air swirling round my body. But I cannot move my legs. Both legs and feet are angled against something solid and icy.

Under the covers I reach down to my feet and draw out a copper hot-water bottle with no residual warmth. It is cold as iron. There is a faint sighing breeze from the open window.

The month is October. I am Bella Strahan and I am in the Royal Victoria Hospital for Tuberculosis.

Around me the other patients are heavily asleep and I have a problem. There is no space on the locker for such a large item as the bottle, even if I could see where to place it in the dark. The floor is too far away for me to drop the thing and risk waking the sleepers. It is my first night here and that would be no way to court popularity.

I place the hard, cold container on the bed while I consider what to do. If I leave it there, I have only to turn over for it to fall off. I am cornered. At last I take off my lacy bed-jacket, a present from my mother meant for sitting up and looking pretty. It was not meant to be slept in, but I had been too cold at lights out to take it off. Now, leaving my arms uncovered, I wrap it round the hard, corrosive metal. Wherever it is placed, the hollowed bed will make sure it finds me and makes icy contact, but the shock will be less savage.

With some determination I take hold of the covers and heave, turning over in the same movement. Ah, that's better. I tuck the cold linen closely round my body.

As I struggle back to oblivion, the breeze rises.

It is 10 a.m. and they are waiting. Knowing that I am to have no breakfast they have allowed me to sleep on, so I am lying here, awake now, like a very thin, very clean, very tense drum, feeling the regular thud of my heart and watching the massive hands of the ward clock go out of focus at every beat.

Respectful allusions are made in hushed voices to my 'induction'. I do not know whether I am vestal virgin or lamb to the slaughter.

Suddenly, with a metallic swish, the day is cut off and I can no longer see the pleasant lawn sloping away from the ward. Close up, too close for comfort, are the enormous orange flowers and bamboo leaves of the privacy curtain. A trolley is thrust through a gap on the window side of the bed, restoring the light, and I am staring at an array of gleaming silver instruments, an orange rubber tube, and an enormous bell jar full of water. The sun shines encouragingly through it, but I am too apprehensive to be cheered by this.

They're doing it *here*, I think, startled. I had been waiting for a summons to the operating theatre assumed to be somewhere nearby. Before I can so much as gulp, three bodies, two doctors and a nurse, squeeze through the curtains and surround the trolley. They are talking as they enter and go on

15

talking before turning to me. The handsome, dark one, Dr. McPherson, gives me a beaming smile and explains briefly why I am here.

'Doesn't take long,' he adds, as he screws together the most enormous hypodermic syringe I have ever seen

'Where does that go?' I ask in fright. It might be bad form to ask but I have to know.

'We get the tip between the chest wall and the outside of the lung,' he answers, rubbing his hands like a magician warming to his subject, 'and introduce air into the cavity with this little chap.' He throws a fond look at the six-inch hypodermic with its three-inch needle. I look at it askance. 'We'll see it doesn't hurt much.'

'What does it do?' I persist.

'Squeezes the lung down to the size of a fist,' he says, 'to rest it. That way there's much less pressure on the affected area. Otherwise any cavity opens and closes with every breath you take and it doesn't get a chance to heal.' He gestures the nurse forward, a tall woman with a starched, frilled cap and an air of command.

'Turn over onto your left side, dear,' she says.

As I turn over, I can see Dr. McPherson attaching the tube to the bell jar and I try to concentrate on what I know about air pressure from my days in the science lab. However hard I try to remove myself, though, I still feel invaded as my arm is gently lifted and the cold swab descends on my underarm area which no one but myself has touched since babyhood. As the needle penetrates my skin, the pain is almost welcome, recalling me to practicalities. Then a feeling of pressure in my chest, neck, back and shoulders mounts until the doctors, who have been muttering inaudibly to each other, sound satisfied and the needle is removed.

As soon as the trio have left and the screens are removed there is a chorus of 'Are you all right?'

'OK then?'

'How did that go?'

I lift my head and wriggle to release the tight covers. 'Fine!' I say. 'Very glad that's over, though.' I am lying in a beam of sunlight feeling new-born, but my pleasure is short-lived.

'What d'you mean "over"?'

A single voice rises above the background chatter. 'You have that done every week for the next three to five years.'

'Sometimes twice a week,' someone else adds. 'We all have it.'

But I hardly hear. My inner voice is screaming in protest and the clock has gone out of focus again.

My mind returns to the events of the past seven months. It was March, in my twentieth year and I was happily engaged on the second year of my literature degree when one day a mobile radiography van came round to test the student population. It was an innocent-looking van, rather like an ambulance, but bigger than usual with sharper corners and a separate cabin for the driver. Although it looked so neutral, like a judge withholding judgement, it was specially equipped inside for quick, revealing chest x-rays, with a screen at one end for privacy when stripping to the waist, and some unfamiliar machinery at the other. Judgements were about to be made. I was positioned against a cold panel and told not to breathe for a few seconds while the x-ray was taken.

There were a few other students there with me. We dressed again and went heedlessly on our way, but by the time the questing vehicle's rounds were finished, seven students were found to be suffering from one or another of the many forms of the disease, of which pulmonary tuberculosis, TB of the lungs, was the most lethal. Seven lives were changed.

At the time I did not know why there was this sudden concentrated interest in finding cases of TB. Certainly it was a dire and deadly disease, but one that had been with us for a very long time. It had always generated hushed voices and secrecy, sad looks and a hand to the mouth, as if its name dare not be spoken. Why now? Of the few people I knew who suffered from it two had died and the outlook for the others was not good. Maybe this new initiative would offer them a better chance.

I assumed it was an area of public concern that had been neglected, like so many others, during the recent war. Indeed it was, but that was not the whole truth. In fact, the government had decanted eight thousand TB patients from sanatoria the length and breadth of the country during the war in expectation that the beds would be needed for wounded soldiers, sailors and airmen as well as civilian casualties. The explosive result was that mortality figures for the disease had shot up almost to the 20% mortality rate of Victorian times at their highest point. The rising death toll was completely out of hand. The most stringent measures were necessary.

Two or three weeks after my x-ray, I set out to attend a hospital appointment. I was to see a senior doctor at the Victoria Dispensary in the unfortunately named Spittal Street. The dispensary was only about a hundred yards from the Co-operative department store, where we bought household goods like our recently purchased dining table. The proximity seemed strange, like seeing a friendly, familiar face wearing a menacing expression. It was with extreme reluctance that I dragged myself past one set of doors and on to the other.

I was ushered into the presence of a doctor with dark, wavy hair and deep lines etched down each cheek and across his forehead. Facing the lighted panel on the wall where the x-ray of my chest was displayed, he lifted a small pointer and I turned to face my mortality. When I was a child, I was always fascinated to see my toe bones, surrounded by the luminous halo that was my flesh, in the machine used to check shoe size. Now here were my ribs, reminding me of the cartoon skeletons that appeared in the weekly comics *The Dandy* and *The Beano*. They were what we had instead of *The Simpsons* and we read them with the same enthusiasm that we now bring to watching Homer and Bart.

The doctor, Dr. Chivers, pointed to a vaguely white area like a little cloud on one side of the x-ray, a cloud from which odd wisps rose at the edge like smoke and, to those who could read it, no doubt carried a message. I could see a semi-circle of smaller white dots strung from one collar-bone to the other just like beads in a necklace. The doctor talked quietly of calcified deposits, which they were, as being the body's attempts at healing itself, leaving me to draw the conclusion that, if they had been successful attempts, I would not be needing his advice.

My heart plummeted. Three-quarters of the academic year had gone and it looked as if it had all been for nothing. If I could not sit my exams there would be no credits. A year wasted. I would have to do all the work again if... I did not allow myself to finish the thought.

Then, Dr. Chivers questioned me further and established that I had no cough which meant that I was unlikely to infect anyone. He said that I could finish my studies for that year before starting serious treatment. I relaxed at this good news and realised that I had been holding my breath. It surprised me that I should have minded the possibly lost months so much when my whole life was at risk, but no one likes to spend time and care on something for absolutely no return. If my life were to be curtailed I certainly did not have time to repeat something that I had already all but done.

My spirits lifted again when he said that my condition had been caught at an early stage and that a few months of bed rest might do the trick and let me get on with my life. I nodded eagerly. I was young and optimistic. If this expert thought I would escape with a few months of suspended living, I was ready to believe him. A few minutes later I was on my feet ready to leave, but after looking me earnestly in the face for a long moment, he made me sit down again. Once he was sure of my full attention, he went over the ground already covered, while my mind made its own, sometimes rebellious, reservations.

'You must rest as much as possible until the long vacation.'

'No outings? No dancing?'

'No! Go to bed early!' he answered sharply. It was clear there was to be no negotiation.

But what do I do after eight o'clock at night? I asked myself, picturing my solitary self beneath the covers listening to the sound of laughter downstairs, and my friends, disconsolate, outside.

'Avoid strenuous physical exercise!'

Good, I thought, someone else will have to do the shopping now.

'You must rest completely in bed during the long vacation!'

What a prospect!

'Drink as much milk as possible!'

Not my favourite tipple.

'Eat as much butter and cheese as possible!'

Hate cheese. Don't like butter much either..

'Eat as much protein as possible!'

So no more vegetarian meals.

'Avoid stressful situations!'

I don't go looking for them; they just find me, I thought soberly.

He then made me promise to obey to the letter every word of advice he uttered. The unspoken subtext was: 'If you want to live.'

I had wanted to cheer up this harassed man and smooth out the lines that life had etched in his face, but had only convinced him that I was not taking things seriously. I left feeling chastened and thinking wryly of the year I had just spent eating vegetarian lunches in the Students' Union Refectory in George Square. Still, nut cutlets had been my usual choice. At least there was some protein in nuts.

On my way home to report to an anxious mother, I wondered whether the cloud that had descended on me was visible to the other travellers, as I stared unseeingly at the busy crowds. Literature, my subject, was a rich source of information on 'consumption', as it was known. I thought about the operatic Mimi in *La Bohème* dying from the loss of her lover, Rudolfo; Marguerite Gautier in *La Dame aux Caméllias* dying tragically just as she discovered that her love was returned; and Katherine Mansfield, just dying with so many stories still untold. Was there no end to the misery engendered by this fatal condition? I felt there must be a better way. Was I really cut out for a romantic heroine, I wondered. Life had handed me a wild card. It was up to me, I thought, how I played it now.

I did not have a long journey to reach home; three miles by municipal bus. If you were a Scottish student at a Scottish university, you were encouraged to attend the institution nearest your home. Although this was sometimes considered ungenerous, I am not complaining. It allowed me to do what I needed to do; totally immerse myself in books in one of the best universities in the world.

Two months later, all my second year exams were over – English language, English literature, Latin and history, all over and done with. Students from far places had ebbed back home and I was back, twenty-four hours a day, in the bosom of my family.

Although it was some years since the war had ended, we were still riding the crest of the wave of optimism that began then. We were all at work or studying. My father was safely home from the Far East and we had settled into family life with two parents again. My elder brother, Ned, was studying at Edinburgh College of Art and I was at Edinburgh University. My younger brother, Laurie, was at George Heriot's School and my young sister, Louise, at Boroughmuir Senior Secondary. Breakfast was grabbed on the hoof, but we enjoyed our evening meal together with a free exchange of views and lots of laughter and, although my recent news had subdued the hilarity, there were much worse places to be.

The bed rest seemed easy enough until a domiciliary specialist visited me. (An attempt was being made to optimise sanatorium beds by encouraging care at home, where and when that was possible.) He was a beautifully groomed and manicured man who perhaps felt a little uncomfortable in his pinstripe suit that was more appropriate for the corridors of power in a large hospital. No doubt he felt even more uncomfortable when he tried to leave through the door of the built-in wardrobe, burying his face in a row of hanging clothes. For some reason I had foreseen this, but was powerless to avert it. I wrestled with both his embarrassment and my own wicked amusement.

He told me that he had decided to include me in an experiment; he believed that an edge could be gained in the fight against TB by increasing the supply of blood to the victim's lungs and his method was to raise the patient's bed at the foot by eighteen inches. So up went the footboard of my bed onto wooden blocks.

The head-down-feet-up position made my neck ache and made books, even paperbacks, extremely heavy. I could manage to hold them for half an hour at a time, but Russian novels such as *War and Peace* or *The Brothers Karamazov* were definitely out. Even without the weight of books my arms would often feel heavy and congested.

Sometimes I resorted to embroidery, with a special danger to add a bit of spice – if I dropped the needle it was more than likely to fall into my eye. In spite of this I completed a supper cloth and a rather summery-looking tea cosy with swathes of flowers in twining green and various shades of gold.

There was a constant tendency to gravitate up the bed, jack-knife at the head end and have to wriggle back, feet first, into the advised position. I only knew that it had happened when I started to have a normal view of things and could see the room laid out in front of me; the small, upholstered chair in vivid tapestry and the dressing-table and book-shelves that Lou and I had painted white with green reeded edging. Usually I just had an extremely boring view of the ceiling.

Pyjamas were the best wear, otherwise my nightdress, obeying the laws of gravity, would end up round my waist or even higher in an uncomfortable mass. Considering the cautions I had been given against exertion and even moving, it was quite a struggle to hoick it down again, or rather *up* to where my feet were.

Louise and I had shared a bedroom for years and now I had it to myself. No more cosy chats at bedtime. No more watching her wriggle across the bed to her own side with closed eyes. No more seeing her vulnerable sleeping face. There was not so much pleasure in having my own room, after all.

During the day the radio was my life-line. Once the sounds of family leaving for work, school and college had died away, along with what passed for busy traffic in our quiet street, and the clamour from the playground of a nearby school had hushed, the wireless took over with *Housewives' Choice.*

It was a request programme faithful to its simple aim of playing music that someone wanted to hear. There was everything from the pop music of the day through grand opera to sacred music, sung both by amateurs and by every trained voice from bass to coloratura soprano and counter-tenor. It was a pleasure to listen to, a painless introduction to the musical world, and it drew a massive audience. It was introduced by a cheerful tune by Jack Strachey called *In a Party Mood* to which one of the presenters, George Elrick, sang his own lyrics, ending with,'I'll be with you all again tomorrow morning...dum-de-diddle, dum-de-diddle, dum-dum-dee.'

Quite often on radio you would be invited back in this way. Henry Hall of *Dance Band* fame would sign off with, 'Here's to the next time!' And most programmes told you what to expect during the coming hour or half hour. *In Town Tonight* began with an excited male voice proclaiming, 'Once more we stop the roar of London's traffic and, from the great crowds, we bring you some of the interesting people who have come by land, sea and air to be In Town Tonight.'

After the first broadcast thousands of people rang the BBC to ask about the opening music. This was tuneful, energetic and jaunty and, for further atmosphere, almost drowned out by the background blare of traffic and street cries. It was the *London Suite* and its composer, Eric Coates, found himself famous overnight. It was all thrilling and involving stuff and gave young people a glimpse of the world they were anxious to enter.

I would have been content to listen to music all day, but my real favourite was the drama then enjoying its heyday. We all revelled in the serials *Paul Temple* and *Dick Barton, Special Agent*. *Paul Temple* was incredibly London-oriented; to its author, Francis Durbridge, Potter's Bar might have been considered 'up north'. The voice of the hero's wife, Steve, played by Marjorie Westbury, fascinated me. It had a very individual timbre, clear, distinct and very easy on the ear. It seemed to breathe opulence and breeding. What a surprise to find then, in a rare actor-before-the-mike snapshot, that she looked plump, cuddly and quite ordinary. The plays themselves, running to several episodes, were detective cases solved with wit and intelligence by the famous pair.

Dick Barton, Special Agent was a cult experience, attracting an audience of 15,000,000 listeners. At 6:45pm, Dick Barton with his henchmen, Jock Anderson and Snowy White, saved the country from ruin in nearly every episode, but it was so thrilling and cleverly done we were all glued to our seats or, in my case, bed. The series had such a hold on the national memory and affection that there have been many attempts to revive it. Films have been made and even a pastiche radio series called *Richard Barton, General Practitioner* in which Dick Barton's supposed son, Richard, a country doctor, tells of his senile father, who is constantly fantasising that he is surrounded by enemies, who must be fought off.

Any play was an exciting listen, but a late afternoon series, an early soap, had a special place in my life: *Mrs Dale's Diary*. It was broadcast at the time of day when things began to feel a little feverish and fretful. The light would be fading but this unexciting drama relaxed me and made me sleepy. During my long spell in bed at home, the million miles between *Mrs Dale's*

Diary and *Shakespeare* shrank and I grew quite fond of the soap's characters, especially Mrs Dale. Her comfortable middle-class voice and the ease with which she instructed the gardener and imposed order on her artificial environment were soothing. This new addiction would have amused my friends of the 1950s, never mind today's more sophisticated listeners, but it took me away from my static life into a different world, a reassuring one where actions were governed by reason.

Cut off from University life, I waited eagerly for visits from friends. They were my second, vital life-line; a living link with reality, although inevitably as time wore on, I found that the animated conversation went on above my head and did not include me. They usually spoke of the strange behaviour of the lecturers we shared. The one who had lost his temper at the late arrival of a student; the one who was now conducting his tutorials in a nearby coffee bar; the one who was skipping lectures, although they could hardly take place without him. We found it all hilarious.

Lecturers were life 'writ large'; intensely individual men and women whose idiosyncrasies brought them under a sometimes distorting spotlight. The lecturer who showed up for two introductory lectures and vanished from the map was possibly having a breakdown, but his students assumed he was out somewhere enjoying himself and did likewise, usually in the Students' Union. The lecturer in Mediaeval Literature, who would get out the map to trace the modern counterpart of Camelot and suggest that Lyonesse was not far away drew a few stifled yawns, but where else would you find such involvement and enthusiasm? Our cool assessments had to be excused on the grounds of our age and ignorance. I laughed with the tale-tellers. I could contribute nothing except laughter. I was a ghost in the land I had recently lived in.

Occasionally, however, I would introduce a friend who was not known to the others and then I would be able to take a more active part in the conversation. The usual hullabaloo was in progress in my bedroom one afternoon in the vacation when my mother appeared with the very caring minister of the church where I was baptized, St. Bernard's in Stockbridge. She went off to make one of many cups of tea and I set about introducing my other visitors to him. Rev. D was a delightful man to talk to and I had hopes of shrinking the generation gap in his company. 'This is George,' I began. 'George is studying science at the Heriot-Watt College.'

George smiled his transforming smile and Mr D nodded, as one professional man to another.

'Cathy,' I singled her out with a nod, 'is doing classics at EU.' A deeper acknowledgment this time. Clergymen approve of classics. 'And Shirley and Helena,' nodding towards Shirley's fair skin and natural curls and Helena's dark, straight crop, 'are doing the M.A. course at EU.' An indulgent, approving smile this time.

Finally I came to my friend, Marie, who had gone further afield than most of us and was attending the London School of Economics at a time when Beatrice Webb was still padding the corridors there.

'And this is Marie,' I said. 'Marie studies in London.'

Oh,' he said with deep sympathy, having completely misheard, 'so Marie's daddy's in London, is he?'

It would have been easier to ignore, if he had not, at the same time, patted her on the head. At five feet eight inches, she was not much below his own height. A flicker of amusement went round every face but his and mine. I managed to take a keen interest in the quilt. Marie was the most sophisticated friend I had and had hit the road to London running.

The cat, Shelley, became a constant companion and did her best to keep life interesting, mainly by sleeping. She spent hours on my bed but seldom joined me before mid-morning so when I woke early one day with something furry tickling my leg, it took a massive effort of will to peel back the covers and investigate.

There she was, lying alongside me, tail beating a slow tattoo against my leg. This was not her normal behaviour. I noticed too that she was staring up at me in a trusting, excited way. I was flattered. It is true that dogs love attention and love to be chosen, but cats are normally the ones to do the choosing. Why had I been chosen? I gave her a closer look and knowledge leapt into my head as if I had taken a bite from the apple. She was about to have kittens.

Sleeping household or no, I yelled for help and my younger brother, Laurie, who had the family tropism towards animals in strong measure, took her away to a more suitable nesting place. He sat by her most of the day, stroking her, while she purred and presented at intervals another little mouth to feed. By evening the family had grown by six new members. She obviously believed, like the poet whose name she shared, in free love.

The cat was not there the day I was threatened by the spider. It was offering to come down its silk rope on to the bed so I fixed my gaze on it to make sure I would see where it landed and could send it on through the open window. I waited for it to come down in vain. As long as I watched, it was static. As soon as I looked away, however, it hurtled down, closing the gap between us. We played this kind of cat-and-mouse game for a long time until we were both tired.

The creature's movements were so clearly defined by my own that I cannot see it as coincidence. I have since heard of a class of boys, set by their science teacher to record the pathways taken by insects in a makeshift maze, who found they could actually direct their charges. Clipshears to the right, millipedes to the left, chuggy pigs straight up the middle! Maybe the Greeks were right and there is more than one God. Maybe we are all exercising powers that we don't even know we have.

In general there was little excitement of an unexpected kind, but I remember one noisy day. It was windy and the sky was full of the flying clouds and gulls that are such a feature of the

Edinburgh sky-scape. Children seem more excitable and shout more. Dogs bark more. We had fastened the flapping muslin curtain to the steel rod for extending the window outwards and I was enjoying watching the fresh air fill the curtain like a spinnaker when a more forceful breeze suddenly billowed the curtain. This lifted the rod right off the catch so that the window was driven against the wall and broke. I watched it come bouncing back with a jagged hole in the bottom segment and heard the mocking tinkle of broken glass as it hit the ground.

My immediate thought was what about the night? I had grown used to the window being open during the day but it was always closed at night. Who, after all, wants to be rained on while asleep?

The chink and clatter of china and cutlery as the soup-plates were placed onto the bed tables on the ward recalled me to the present. The five months of bed rest at home had not improved things and the new academic session was well under way without me. Now I was on Younger Ward with a newly collapsed lung and windows open day and night.

I looked round at the expectant faces, mostly smiling, as they waited for my reaction and my mind adjusted to these new circumstances. I hadn't bargained for the weekly stabbing sessions that they were telling me about, but so be it. If other people survived it then so could I. I looked round at my ward-mates curiously, exactly as they were looking at me.

We were going to be together for some time.

CHAPTER 2
Cold Comfort

'Well, not so bad as yesterday, I'd say.' Meg Richie was sitting up in bed, well enough muffled for the ski-slopes in a thick-knit sweater with thick-knit deer browsing across her bosom.

I was not so sure. I had poked one hand out of the bedclothes to drink my breakfast tea and nibble a slice of toast and now it was purple again. I had tried warming it on my hot water bottle but that was now tepid. I needed to become as inured to the cold as my ward-mates seemed to be. I had not been warm once in the fortnight of my stay here.

Exposure to the full rigour of a British winter was part of the grand plan. Freezing the bacillus out of existence with or without freezing the patient in the process was the idea. 'Every shiver is worth a guinea' was the stark message that the patient was expected to support.

I had always hated the cold. The seven years of war-time austerity when the coal ration had stretched to only one fire per household so that the bedrooms were always cold had been bad enough. We woke in winter to a thick coating of ice inside the windows and were glad of the glass between us and the elements. Now there was not even an ice-coated window.

Yesterday morning we had been wakened as usual at 5:30 to the clatter of enamel basins and steaming water jugs. The sky was the deepest midnight blue. It was the one and only time in any twenty-four hours that we were allowed to close the windows because we were about to strip to the waist to wash, but the permission to close them died on the nurse's lips. She was staring at our beds.

'"Too late, too late," shall be the cry,' Maisie Chapman muttered.

I hardly heard her. I was trying to make sense of the soft, white blanket that someone had laid on my bed – on all our beds.

'Snow-in-summer,' someone remarked.

Well, hardly summer. It *was* October. But snow? I reached out to touch its soft purity, moving my knee in the process, and a small crevasse opened, showing the beige bed-cover beneath. I moved my cramped feet and legs, but the icy blanket stayed intact for the next four hours until at 9:30 the ward-maid flapped the top covers, decanting it onto the floor. As part of the cold cure, there was no central heating and fires were lit only for the two hours of visiting time three days a week. The pile of snow lay unmelted in front of the empty grate until it was swept up a couple of hours later. It was so cold that the solid crystals of ice kept their snow-flake integrity and were no threat to the expensive wooden floor.

'They wouldn't have believed this in Belsen!' said Betty Shiels in the bottom bed.

I winced at the inept comparison. Our lives were not comfortable, but the inmates of war-time Belsen would have given much to change places with us. We were not being starved, beaten, overworked, shot or gassed. Nevertheless the weather was not mild. My hands tightened on my tepid bottle beneath the blankets.

'I have been in the snow.'

There was a stirring of interest. We had all, of course, been in the snow at some time, but the novelty now was the speaker,

30

the newest admission to the ward. And not so very new; she had been with us for five days now and so far had not said a word.

All heads in the ward turned as one towards the speaker, a young, slender girl with soft, dark hair and hazel eyes. She hailed from one of the Hebridean islands. It was almost our first look at the face that had lain buried between pillows and covers for the best part of a week and we drank in what the newcomer was offering with the passion of sojourners in a land where little happened.

It was an intelligent face, pared down to high cheek-bones and forehead and a well-defined, rather determined chin. In spite of its sharp planes, Mary McKenzie did not look sick. Her skin was pale, without the hectic flush to be seen in advanced cases of the illness.

At first, on her arrival, her nearest neighbours had made hesitant offers of books, magazines or sweets, but there had been no sign that she had even heard the friendly voices. There had been no response. Besides there had been a complicity in Sister's manner as she herded the newcomer into bed late one night with whispered words that had left the whole ward a little in awe. We had heard from one of the ward maids that the new patient was a nurse. She was left alone.

How would you cope with that? To be an angel ministering to the sick one day and the next day on the receiving end, your life in danger, unfit to be near your patients. I had often wondered whether the nurses and doctors developed a special immunity. Now I could see they were not fireproof.

But come to that, how did we, the patients, cope with our situation? We were all investing in a myth by being here, the myth of successful treatment, the hope that the medics knew what they were doing, that taking their advice would mean restoration. On the surface we coasted along, lulling our fears to sleep with the knowledge that any change would be long term, any progress would be slow. We tried not to think beyond this point, but sometimes during the night doubt and anxiety squirmed like worms in a can. During the day, ironic jokes brightened the air, but our night thoughts were of the cold, the knife, collapsed lungs, taking the evil-tasting medicine, staying very still. Now here was a sufferer where a healer had been. We did not know what to say.

'Where was that then?' asked Maisie, upper torso exposed to the cold, hands tucked beneath pyjama-clad thighs for warmth. Although less than voluble, she often gave the lead in our shrunken world. As the secretary of a city businessman, she had achieved independence, maturity and the odd holiday abroad, by no means a common event in the 1950s. She appeared to have been in the sanatorium for so long that she knew all there was to know about the treatments. We listened to her.

'On the island,' came the soft, shy response.

I thought I could picture it by relocating the rows of red-blanketed beds on the verandahs of the City Hospital in Edinburgh to a hospital on a remote island. I assumed she was describing a sanatorium, but I was wrong.

'I thought all TB hospitals were on the mainland,' Meg volunteered.

'Oh, they are. It wasn't in hospital,' said Mary, her voice tailing away as if she had already said too much.

'Where then?' persisted Betty.

'It was in school.'

'In school?' Maisie asked.

Jenny Carter, a fourteen-year-old in the next ward, had been in hospital for four years and had never had a lesson since her admission. Her education stopped short even of the eleven-plus exam.

'TB patients here don't get any schooling,' Maisie said in a puzzled way. The Highlands and Islands were supposed to be an impoverished area. How come *they* could provide lessons?

Maybe her voice sounded a little sharp, incredulous. The newcomer looked uncomfortable. What was intended as an amusing comment was turning into an inquisition.

'You see, we were not patients,' she said gently.

'Ordinary, everyday school – for everybody?' I asked, just to be sure.

She nodded.

'You mean the snow came in the open windows of the school?' pressed Betty.

'No, we sat on chairs outside. Kept our gloves on. Sometimes we had to wipe the seats clear of snow to sit down.'

'What for?' Betty asked.

'The wet, of course!'

'No, I meant why the open-air lessons in winter?'

'Oh, it was all the time, not just winter. It was lovely in summer.'

I imagined stretches of green and blue moorland, the calls of birds, the fishing nets, a warm, soft breeze off the sea.

'For crying out loud!' Betty came back to the question that was still puzzling us all. 'Surely you needed to be *inside* with snow on the ground!'

'It was Miss McLeod, you see,' Mary said patiently. 'And it never lasted long.' Her voice had become misty, distant, an echo of itself, as if nothing ever lasted long.

'What about Miss McLeod?' Meg was relentless.

'She was eccentric,' Mary said, and shuddered as a balk of snow slithered off the roof, showering her in passing.

The lawn stretched still white in front of us, criss-crossed with bird tracks. A hundred yards away a stretch of pinewood closed in our quiet world. We were marooned, suspended in a white limbo.

A sharp breeze stirred the quiet, cold air of the ward and all heads turned towards the door where Nurse Robson, Peggy to her intimates, struggled to push a large trolley through the opening.

Its wooden superstructure, with a sloping lid on either side, had a bland, polished surface furnished with keyholes and was hiding the next treat on the agenda.

'Medicines, anyone?' Peggy asked brightly.

33

CHAPTER 3
Drowsy Syrups

Peggy Robson was a slender, auburn-haired mother of three. But for the war she would have been at home, as mothers were in those days, but her naval lieutenant husband had gone down with his ship towards the end of hostilities, leaving her with an inadequate pension and four mouths to feed. Her duties in the sanatorium included dispensing medicines and serving meals and took her from ward to ward, so that she was always in the open air and always wore her navy woollen cloak with crossed straps over the chest, looking like nurse Edith Cavell.

Now, as she held up a pint bottle of medicine, a communal groan rose from the bottom of the ward.

'I PAS,' declared Dawn in the bottom bed, producing a further groan at the over-used pun. As the tot-sized glasses were raised, the glassless few urged, 'Down the hatch!' It was a reassuring ritual.

'Why do you treat us like this?' was asked silently in mock exasperation on one side.

'For your own good!' with pursed lips on the other.

I was glad to be excused. I had previously taken the liquid PAS (para-amino salycilic acid), which could lift the polish off a piece of furniture in a single application, and it had badly affected my stomach and bladder. It had left me with mixed memories, though primarily of gratitude to the fairly new National Health Service. Our family G.P. informed us that the medicine cost £3 per bottle and I had been prescribed two a week: two pints of medicine, six small glasses daily. The cost of this in 1950 was not far below my parents' weekly income and would have been impossible for us to afford without the National Health Service.

Before the NHS was established most people paid a modest contribution for fairly limited medical treatment. It was perfectly possible to over-run your entitlement and I remember one year, when all four of us children had had mumps and chicken-pox, my mother was told we could not have any more treatment unless we could pay cash.

This state of niggardly provision had created a family pecking order for medical care that was logical, but caused problems. The needs of the father would come first because, if the breadwinner was away from work, whether from sickness or accident, there would be no money coming in. (At this time it was emphatically not the practice for married women to go out to work.) Even so, many men took quite foolhardy risks to avoid needless expense.

I remember one lunch-time as a child. My father was sitting at the dining table looking quite pale, his uneaten meal in front of him. My elder brother had got off his chair to pick something up from the floor and when he straightened up he announced, with a frightened face, 'Mum, Daddy's shoes are full of blood.'

My father had been crossing the park on the way home and had climbed the spiked railings to shorten his journey without realising they were slippery. He had ended up impaled with one spike in the groin area. He never explained how he freed himself but he seemed bent on believing that his accident could escape our notice. If the NHS had been in place, he would have been taken straight to hospital. As it was, my mother's nursing skills came to the rescue, as they often did. She was liberal with the iodine bottle and bandages. A whole bandage went into the wound as a dressing. I don't think my father even missed a day at work.

In terms of claims to medical care, children followed on from the breadwinner. In those days, people had a robust attitude to children's ailments, but there were plenty of killer germs out there and then they were vulnerable. Diphtheria, whooping cough, scarlet fever, measles, mumps and many more were real life or death challenges. Since then, thankfully, their sting has been drawn by inoculation, vaccination and antibiotics. Without these modern initiatives life would be a far riskier proposition.

The perennial danger to children from infectious diseases meant that mothers put themselves at the end of the queue for medical care. Cancers, leaking wombs, varicose veins and ulcers were all ignored for as long as possible, making these severe conditions difficult, lengthy or impossible to cure. Sometimes a mother died from putting treatment off, leaving the family in the direst straits.

I imagine that in the days before the NHS the more expensive treatments available for serious conditions were never even offered to people who could not afford them. Most people were more than grateful for a service that met serious medical needs as well as providing them with glasses and teeth when they were needed.

In the decade before its establishment, holding onto a set of teeth was problematic and there was a tradition of deliberately having all the teeth removed once the gaps were numerous enough to be unsightly. People would have to save hard to afford a replacement set from the dentist before the NHS took the financial strain. The new NHS utopia meant not only more smiles in place but better oral health. The rate of mouth cancer decreased dramatically compared to that in countries without a health service.

When you consider, too, the extended reading life bestowed by a pair of spectacles, easily acquired under the NHS, it is clear that the post-war government had added a possible twenty years of comfort to the average life.

From 1948 on we lived in a newly beneficent society, so I was grateful for my two bottles of PAS and for the heroic but futile efforts to make the hideous stuff more palatable by a choice of flavourings – chocolate, orange and one so horrible it has produced a mental block; maybe peppermint.

Over the following year the medication would be presented in rice-paper sachets the size of a two pence piece, or a half-crown in old money. They were, however, much thicker. The trick was to allow the sachet to get moist in your mouth and swallow it quickly before it could come apart and release its vile powder. If you had less than enough spit, the rice-paper capsule became sticky rather than moist and you were in trouble. Fortunately, when I was once more on this medication, I managed to swallow my sachets, even if it took several goes. Patients were not always successful in this and it is on record that, in a certain sanatorium, the grand piano was found to be full of sachets of PAS hidden by patients who had had more than they wanted of it.

Before I was admitted to the Victoria, I had a series of injections of streptomycin which had to be administered by my mother, who had given up nursing when she married. It was twenty-five years since she had handled a hypodermic needle and seeing her hesitation and apprehension during the first few injections revealed this rock-like, central figure of my life in a new light. I had seldom seen her less than certain about anything and realized that mothers must often pretend, in front of their children, to a confidence that they are far from feeling.

The streptomycin affected my hearing and balance centre so that from then on walking without falling over became a challenge and a balancing act. For many years, even decades, after this therapy, I found walking in the dark not only difficult but dangerous and it is not without hazard even now. I would be dazzled and disabled by the lights of oncoming traffic and would find myself, after the lights had passed, teetering on the edge of the pavement, ready to step into the traffic, drawn by some change in my body. I could neither help nor resist this progress towards the light any more than the moth can.

The doctors were now, after the PAS and streptomycin, waiting to see how my body reacted – in punishing the tubercle bacillus, that is. Any other reaction seemed to be considered fairly irrelevant. It is a measure of the desperation that went with the disease that these unwanted and often permanent side effects were taken lightly by the doctors. It was not unusual for streptomycin to leave the patient stone deaf or suffering from a permanently impaired balance centre, but the pleasure in confirming your hold on life was shared by doctor and patient alike.

'So going from sun to shadow makes you fall over? Take more water with it!'

'Can't walk a straight line? No more tight- ropes for you then!'

'What's that? Can't hear what I'm saying? Join the club and watch my lips!'

At the time of my treatment, safe but effective dosages were still being worked out. I think that later patients were probably better served in this respect than we were. It is well that they were. An early assessment, recently discovered, lists other side effects as nausea, vomiting, loss of appetite, muscle weakness, persistent diarrhoea, bleeding, bruising, rapid heartbeat, changes in urine, fatigue, thrush, rash, itching, swelling, dizziness and breathing problems.

My knowledge of these reactions to streptomycin was some way into the future. Few of us at the time knew of the unsteady walk as we were on strict bed rest, even to the ministering of bed pans. I fared worse than most patients in this. Privileges like walking to the bathroom had to be earned by gaining weight, but I never did. I left the Victoria weighing the same seven stone, two pounds that I had weighed on my arrival. By the time the medics admitted defeat and let me up to wash and use the toilet, my legs were like very long, very thin bananas or, as my mother graphically put it, 'porridge spirtles.' I walked like Bambi on ice until I became stronger and learned to negotiate changes between sun and shade and how to graduate my own movements. It was not a good idea to turn my head quickly unless I was prepared to find myself sitting on the pavement.

Records showing evidence of tuberculous decay go back to its discovery in the spinal columns of Egyptian mummies from around 2,400 BC. The Greek physician, Hippocrates, the Father of Medicine, named it the worst disease of his time because it was nearly always fatal, so our doctors' light-hearted responses to unwanted side-effects could be interpreted as the scent of victory in a prolonged battle against an old, ferocious and intractable enemy. Not only were the patients given the medication not dead, they were showing signs of recovery.

On my ward in the sanatorium, we had a ready measure of how things used to be. Nurse Lucie, who might have been about sixty years old, had been a patient in the Victoria when she was my age and was the only survivor out of the hundred patients then in the hospital. She was a very stoic figure with permanently rolled-up sleeves, a purposeful but thoughtful manner, and an unhurried pace. Was it fanciful in me to sense a fierce loneliness in this indomitable woman? Having never moved out of the ghetto of TB care, she must have felt like a very distant outpost of empire as the sun of her own life started declining.

She put her survival down to raw eggs in orange juice, a wicked brew as I could later testify. The resemblance of this to prairie oysters suggests a different Nurse Lucie from the one we knew; someone from a privileged, moneyed background, living a wildly high life perhaps. But her age would have placed her birth firmly in the last decade of Victoria's reign, when young women did not need prairie oysters. They were the restorative of the flapper age of short, fringed dresses, lipstick and long cigarette-holders, an entire world war away from Nurse Lucie's girlhood, and so her pick-me-up must have been medical or nutritional, not the result of wild living.

TB is a great leveller. All classes of people fall victim to it, but it is fashionable to see it as a disease of poverty and overcrowding, and of course the infection spreads more rapidly in these conditions. By the 1950s, 90% of the population were considered to have been in contact with the bug and, for the most part, to have produced the antibodies needed to repel it. Those who succumb have no means of fighting the bacillus because they have no antibodies. This explains why one person in a family might succumb while others manage to remain healthy. My personal feeling is that it is a disease in which discouragement plays a part. There was plenty of discouragement in my life at the time of diagnosis, at least more than I could handle, and also a strange, knowing melancholy. Without a symptom of the disease – no cough, no spit, no blood – I was waiting for the blow to fall, while telling myself not to be ridiculous.

Moneyed people would simply go abroad for their health, often to Switzerland or some other place where the air was clear and pure. They would live well and take life easy until they felt and were pronounced better. Needless to say they fared no better in most cases than the land-locked poor. Their lives may have been a little longer but still fell pretty short of three-score years and ten. Nurse Lucie, in her own context, was unique. She was one in a hundred.

TB is predominantly a disease of the young and this gives it untold poignancy. It attacks when the young person has survived the hazards of childhood and life is laid out for the taking. The large number of writers and artists whose lives were cut short by TB, and the treatment of the disease in literature and opera, all served to create an aura of pathos and romanticism surrounding the illness that was a long way from its reality. The deaths from TB amongst writers alone form a frightening roll-call: Franz Kafka, Anton Chekhov, Robert Louis Stevenson,

Katherine Mansfield, D.H. Lawrence, George Orwell, Thomas Mann, W.E. Henley, G. Bramwell-Evans and of course the Brontes – Ann, Emily and Charlotte – who wrote their powerful novels while they waited in bleak certainty for death. Their elder siblings, Maria and Elizabeth, had already died in childhood.

John Keats, the nineteenth-century poet, is a memorable example. Having lost his mother to TB in his teens, he then nursed his young brother, Tom, through the same terminal illness in his early twenties. Within months of Tom's death, Keats himself had a haemorrhage from the lungs that announced his death sentence. The supreme emotional power of his sonnets, as he faced death, comes partly from this sad knowledge. He felt that his destiny was being denied him and asked bitterly to be remembered as 'One whose name was writ in water.'

Sometimes the heightened drama produced unnecessary fear. The poet, Dylan Thomas, believed for a lifetime, albeit not a long one, that he suffered from consumption, but x-rays taken after his death at the age of forty-two proved that he was not affected.

Near the peak of the TB epidemic in Victorian Britain, the cull of the general population was terrifying. In the year 1838 alone, just before Victoria was crowned, over 59,000 people in Britain died from consumption. That is well over 1,000 deaths for every week of the year. In the years between 1850 and 1910 in Great Britain 4,000,000 people died of tuberculosis. That is on average 66,666 deaths annually. No wonder the condition has had such an enormous impact on the collective psyche!

However, on a certain Saturday evening in 1950 in a ward in the Victoria Hospital, none of us knew all of this. We were keeping a watching brief on Nurse Peggy Robson. Saturdays were special. The visitors had come and gone, we had had our evening drink – cocoa or Ovaltine – and were all deeply involved in a play in the series *Saturday Night Theatre*. I had noticed – we all had – that Peggy spent less time on the female

41

ward than on the male one and that evening we were particularly aware of the men's amused voices and Peggy's girlish giggles.

We got back to the play where the female lead, recently a bride, had just found a bottle of peroxide that suggested her groom might be the serial killer who was terrorising the countryside. It was at this crucial point that the shared radio, under the control of the nursing staff in the Duty Room (on this occasion Peggy) was switched savagely over to *Jack Jackson's Record Roundup*, leaving us gasping with suspense while a deep voice sang:

> *You make me feel so young.*
> *You make me feel there are songs to be sung,*
> *Bells to be rung*
> *And a wonderful spring to be sprung...*

We looked at one another in dismay. No one did anything. It was no good calling out protests; we were not supposed to shout. But there was a wonderful spring to be sprung and I sprang it by leaping out of bed. I was going, whatever the cost, to switch the programme back on again. But I forgot that I was still connected to the bed by the headphones and was dragged back onto the blankets with a strangled cry. I became part of the shrieking hilarity that ended our day.

The laughter from next door had stopped. The violent release of tension in our ward had discharged itself first in an enormous screech of laughter, followed by cascades of giggles that must have had a tonic effect, but later, when the ward was dark and quiet, I found my pillow wet and wondered whether others wept at night like me, in silence beneath the covers.

CHAPTER 4
We'll go no more a-roving

One of the keenest deprivations of our altered state was that, if something reduced you to tears, there was nowhere to cry – except under the blankets. No one would pry, but everyone was free to speculate on the cause of your distress.

This tacit agreement was the best solution under the circumstances, but intimacies were often stifled in the process and deeper friendships that might have blossomed were stillborn. Relationships were cordial but generally not very deep. We were united in a bond of common experience up to a point; there was solidarity, but the real friendships that I made while on the ward were all the result of one-to-one encounters where only two of us were present.

Something that has struck me only recently is the extent to which life in the sanatorium was a process of continued relinquishment. You gave up a normal daily routine for another that was more regimented and less comfortable, but hopefully restorative. You gave up your right to protest at the limits that were placed on your movements and your activities and at the regular invasion of your body by needles and tubes. You gave up your right to any meaningful privacy. You went on making sacrifices to necessity, paring down your life until what was left was a determined hanging on, a waiting for an upturn in fortune.

Sometimes the sacrifice was one in which you had no say. We all accepted the gradual but relentless falling off in the numbers of our visitors. We had no way to keep them other than through mutual friendship and compassion, or shared memories of good times in the past. But young people live in the future and they soon became bored with the lack of movement in the sanatorium. I missed the interplay between friends I once knew well, but who now came singly or in pairs to see me. I missed being one of a circle.

Now I belonged to a different circle, where we were defined by the names of our illnesses, the methods of treatment, and who treated us. Some of the staff had nicknames and we had acronyms for the various brands of operations undergone. It felt like being back at school.

The one place free of visitor fatigue was the sheltered environment you grew up in, the heart of the family. 'Home,' as the poet Robert Frost once said, 'is the place that, when you go there, they have to take you in.' Now we could no longer go there, but home was brought to us in willing hands laden with fruit, flowers, books, magazines, sweets (when they could be had), fresh pyjamas, sweaters, combs, shampoo; the million and one things that make life bearable. More important were the faces above the hands, beaming warmth and hope, counselling the patience that we did not have. This was why, when I did have a say in the outcome, I lost George.

George was a friend of the longest standing. We had been at school together since the age of five and we lived, for at least thirteen years, less than a hundred yards apart. When my family moved, it was only another couple of hundred yards away.

I had kept an anxious eye on George in primary school, helped or hindered him with his stammer by willing him to get the words out, and wished a speedy end on the teacher who harassed him, Miss A of the tiger-eye beads and striped woollen dress – an aging wasp in sheep's clothing.

At High School our paths diverged. I went to Boroughmuir Senior Secondary School, George went to Broughton. In spite of the broad-based Scottish Higher Leaving Certificate curriculum – or maybe because of it – our choice of subjects polarised into arts subjects for me, science subjects for George.

We did not know this, however, as we did not meet up again until the next stage, university for me, national service, followed by more study, for him. He chose to spend the statutory two years' service in the air force, but nearly came to a sticky end when his parachute roman-candled, failing to open until he was just a few feet from the ground. The jolt to his spine as it did so was enough to see him into hospital for a time. His 'para' days were over, but in compensation for negligence over the faulty parachute, he was shuffled sideways into a position as aide-de-camp to a top figure in post-war Berlin.

Yes, the war was over, but we were still clearing up. The atrocities of Belsen, Dachau, and Auschwitz remained raw in our memories. It was impossible not to weep at the living skeletons shown on newsreels at the cinema picking lice from their clothing and eating those minimal scraps of protein because they were starving. Impossible to remain dry-eyed at the pictures of bulldozers shovelling mounds of bodies into a communal grave. In the process often an arm or leg would make a lifelike movement or a face would seem not to have the total blankness of the dead. Indeed a few people were found alive amongst their dead companions.

Trials for war crimes were still going on. We were still fixated on the exploits that brought the war to an end, but apprehension was shifting to the future of atomic power, which might, as some saw it, see an end to the human race. After the mass slaughter of Hiroshima and Nagasaki, who could blame them? The human race had moved on from the single combat of, say, the biblical David and Goliath, to where it was possible for one man to press a single button and kill 300,000 human beings without having to look them in the eye. But in spite of the searing time we had been through and the uncertainty of the future, we had hopes of creating a better world. We were looking forward.

I am ashamed to say that at this distance in time I do not remember how George and I came together again, but I remember him, as a second-year student, telling me about his war exploits over a cup of coffee in an Edinburgh department store. Little attention was given in those days to students as a separate community or their special needs and we just had to be satisfied with snowy white tablecloths, crisp rolls and butter, and dainty iced or cream cakes. Not too difficult on the whole.

To me it was not a case of love at even second sight, perhaps more of a desire for protective coloration. Earlier boy-friends had been kept at a distance because I was determined to finish my course with a degree. My parents had sacrificed a great deal to keep me at university even with the bursary or grant that became available. At a time when there was little or no possibility of family planning, marriage was not an option. Marriage meant children and I still had to rule the world.

Besides, I liked the world that university had opened up. I wanted to know all there was to know about Shakespeare, Christopher Marlowe, John Donne, Andrew Marvell, Tennyson, Browning and Byron, as well as the Brontes, George Eliot and Jane Austen, in all their blazing singularity, and I couldn't do it through *Woman's Own* or even the local library. I had to know where to look, which buttons to press.

Now suddenly, halfway through my course, people were pairing off. George had left his stammer somewhere in his past and felt like a comfortable, slightly flamboyant option. And, of course, he looked very handsome in uniform. I wanted to get to know him better.

In this I was not disappointed. No one could have been more attentive or supportive – and this went all the way from warming my frozen hands back to life in a Pentland blizzard to supplying books, visits, jokes, presents and stories from the laboratory. He passed on to me the more sensational medical details of the background to tuberculosis. It was from him I learned that the tubercle bacillus, under the microscope, can hardly be told apart from the organism that causes leprosy and that leprosy too was once endemic in Europe.

Visitors to old churches will be aware of how many of these ancient buildings have a leper's *squint*, a small slit of window through which a leper might 'join' in a church service from outside in the open air without being a threat to the rest of the congregation. And viewers of the film *Braveheart* will remember that Robert the Bruce's father suffered from this dread disease and was never seen in public.

Lepers were traditionally relegated to an area well outside the village or town they had once lived in. Such areas had their own give-away names but time often laid a gentler and disguising hand on them. Liberton, for instance, a district to the south of Edinburgh, has nothing to do with liberty or freedom. It was the settlement or tun (town) of the leper.

It shocked me recently to read of a district in a third world country where orphans born with HIV were cast out without support to starve to death. And starve they would have done without a nearby leper colony that took them in. It is equally shocking to find that leper colonies still exist. The disease has been curable since the mid-1950s, but such benefits of civilization are not readily transferred to the developing countries. If you have to fall victim to a disease with a brutal history and a long obituary list, like tuberculosis or leprosy, there are worse places to do it than a major city in a recently flourishing empire. Needless to say, in 1950 I was not aware of how extremely lucky we all were.

I thanked my lucky stars for George and got more and more attached to him during my months of bed rest at home. He showered time, presents and attention on me and made me laugh. He glued me to the future, a future foreshadowed in one of our outings before I was admitted into the Victoria.

I had had the tell-tale x-ray in March of 1950 and was to be permitted to take my annual exams in May of that year before starting treatment for my condition. The May holiday lay in between. It was the spring of the year and we decided to trek the five miles or so into the Pentland Hills with a picnic.

Edinburgh didn't seem to be suffering from global or any other warming at that time and, in deference to my mother's nursing streak, I was wearing a pair of crocheted cotton gloves and a light coat. The old-world village of Swanston was our target, chosen by George, perhaps as a nod towards my literary leanings. For a large part of his boyhood it had been the holiday home of Robert Louis Stevenson.

We set out at a brisk pace and covered several miles without noticing, because we were so engrossed in conversation but, as we left the last suburban houses behind us and set off into the foothills, we were overtaken by a fierce blizzard. The tender green of the new-fledged trees was overlaid with slant white needles, a dramatic and weirdly beautiful sight. In a matter of minutes, hail lay thick all around us and we decided to shelter under a tree and eat.

My hands were numb in the green cotton gloves and I tried to ease them off by nipping the tips between my teeth and pulling, but stopped when I realized I was biting my fingers and there was no feeling in them. George came to the rescue and between us we got my hands free. He set about rubbing my bloodless, white digits in an attempt to restore the circulation.

I could see what the next step would be. How could we avoid it? The romantic aria from La Bohème, as Mimi and Rudolfo meet for the first time. '*Your tiny hand is frozen, let me warm it into life.*'

First he hummed it thoughtfully, while I looked down on his bent, dark head. Then he whistled it cheerfully, surely a first. Still no change. Although I could feel the warmth of his hands above my wrists, I felt nothing below them. My own efforts, breathing on my fingers and from time to time plunging them inside my coat, were equally useless. Finally he burst into the

48

Italian *Che gelida manina* in a fine, lyric tenor, looking soulfully into my eyes while I pretended to swoon.

'It's not good if we can't get the blood back pretty soon,' he said at last and we decided to turn for home. We never made it to the tiny, historic haven of Swanston.

Trying to recapture the mood of that day, I can see I could have felt justified in thinking that fate was not on our side, but in fact we were full of high hopes and high spirits and had every faith in the future. We were, perhaps, foolish. We were young.

Over the next few months George was a regular and frequent visitor. I passed my exams and life subsided into an unexciting routine of tranquil boredom punctuated by his visits. My mother used to joke about having him move his bed in. When I moved to the Royal Victoria, however, there was a sea change. At home we had privacy, since my siblings all had their own lives to get on with and had no overwhelming desire to hold my hand twenty-four hours a day. Here, with other patients and their visitors around us, we had none. I was not complacent and often found myself wondering whether and how his dedication could stand the test of time and thrive on so little. How long could he wait for us to move on?

His perseverance had stood the test of time for more than a year when the answer came. On the previous Saturday I had had quite a number of visitors who had chatted for a bit then left in ones and twos until only George and my mother remained. Neither seemed inclined to leave the other behind and each was perhaps holding out for a few words alone with me. In the end, the conversation faltered and, at a glance from the nurse on duty, they left together. It made me realize to what extent he was now an accepted member of the family.

The post on Tuesday morning, however, told a different story. A letter from George told me that he had been disappointed and frustrated that he had not been able to see me alone and felt disinclined to visit again unless a change could be made. I don't know what he thought I could do from my position of supreme impotence.

I thought of my mother, who was agoraphobic, and how she must have screwed up her courage to make the journey across town to see me. I thought about the neighbour, surely mistaken in her assumptions, who had seen him in close company with another girl, and saw that she might not be mistaken at all. I thought about George, pulled towards life but stopped in his tracks. I thought about myself and how angry I was at being handed such an ultimatum.

I rummaged in the handbag he had given me and found a fountain pen and wrote to him, explaining that I was unwilling to upset my mother by suggesting that she miss or even cut short any of her visits. I did not explain how rare and valuable they were. I thanked him for his friendship and support and added that we might some time meet again in better circumstances.

It was done. The main thought in my mind now was how to get through the next few hours. What would I do without his sudden startling smile? My throat tightened and my eyes filled with tears. My one thought was that no one should see this.

By inches I submerged myself below the covers, pulling them over my head. Under the blankets it was psychological ground zero, as I got down to mourning my loss and confronting my new, slimmed-down life. In these circumstances the foetal is the only position.

Yet in an odd way the severed bond was almost a relief. For the split second of the decision, I had felt larger than life, justified, elemental. This did not last; of course it didn't. You can't dislodge someone who has been central to your life for such a long and crucial time as if you were removing a splinter from under your nail. But I could now admit to myself that I had felt uneasy since hearing our neighbour's scrap of gossip. She was not a malicious woman. I had begun to wonder if I had become an obstacle instead of a promise, so there was some relief in not carrying such a strong sense of obligation.

If I could have waited until rest hour at two o'clock before ducking below the blankets, no one would have known about the crisis, but tears would not be tears if we could control them.

When I surfaced an hour later, Maisie's eyes were on me. Later still, when gastric tests were in progress and we were left alone together, she looked anxiously across the ward and simply asked, 'George?'

I nodded. She nodded back in sympathy and understanding. It was a look that said 'Par for the course'. I had entered a new freemasonry.

CHAPTER 5
Doctors and Patients

Life in the sanatorium followed a well-worn pattern. At the top of the tree was the consultant, a professor, who gave out dictates from on high and the chances were that, though his finger was theoretically on your pulse, you might never see him.

Beneath him was another shadowy, superintendent figure, Dr E, also issuing edicts to the ranks, but sometimes doing it in person. You did not always like what he had to say. When he told a young girl that she looked rosy as an apple outside with her pink cheeks, but was rotten inside, the hearer looked in vain for kindness, sympathy or any healing balm in the words. Similarly it was not helpful when he asked one long-stay patient whether she would like to go home for Christmas, then told her, 'Not this year, but maybe next.' In years to come I would be surprised to discover that these unkind exchanges, along with other sanatorium traditions, took place over a wide area and seemed to be designed to terrify the patient into submission and into becoming resigned to an inevitably restricted life.

Offering up the evidence for the deliberations of their superiors in regular report sessions were Dr McPherson, a dark, burly figure with a friendly manner, and the hospital registrar,

Dr Kennedy, a young, slim man with glasses, tousled black hair and twinkling eyes.

Sister Cruikshank of the starched uniform and frilled bonnet was always a figure of authority at surgical procedures and manned the interface between troublesome patients and dedicated staff with commendable aplomb. Once, after the weekly refill of air into the pleural cavity, I left the room feeling that things were not quite right. (Refills were given to replace the air absorbed by the lung during the past week and would keep the lung from reflating). I didn't normally react to the treatment beyond a slight constriction of my chest but this time the whole of my right side felt hot and swollen. I reached the waiting-room, only a few paces away, with my arm already lifting from my side as my torso visibly swelled. To my alarmed eye it seemed to reach the size of a football in seconds and I felt that something had to be done.

I walked back into the surgery fearful of being ticked off by the peppery sister and wasn't disappointed. I held up my arm to show the problem.

'Oh,' she said, 'you have a little haematoma,' handed me a plug of cotton-wool and waved me away again. Funnily enough, I found her dismissive manner reassuring, although I did wonder what a *big* haematoma would have been like.

Although I allowed myself to be reassured, we were all, apparently, skating on very thin ice. It was not many months later, on arriving for an air refill, that I found a clutch of fellow patients standing in a huddle and looking quite subdued and asked them what was wrong. They seemed not to want to tell me at first, but finally muttered that someone had died on the table only days before. I mentally took a deep breath to brace myself. It was no good panicking. The success of our treatment depended on carrying on with it, deaths or no. All the same, it was a shock to know that such a thing could happen.

'Oh well,' I said, 'we do have the best, gentlest, most competent doctor in the san.'

'He was the one responsible,' they said.

The doctor, poor man, was 'let go' immediately. The event was a double tragedy. The doctor in question was a young man, whose hopeful career had come to an end or at least been severely checked, invalidating six years of study. But for the patients this was reassuring in a way. If someone was at fault, it meant that the death was not something so random that it could easily happen again. All the same, the atmosphere in the refill clinic remained subdued for weeks after this event. No one whistled or hummed. The chatter was sporadic.

We were in the pavilion or butterfly wards, so called because they were like two 'wings' joined at a shallow angle in the middle, where the duty room and bathrooms were situated. The nursing hierarchy included two more Sisters, one for each of the three wards which were endowed by flourishing Scottish brewers, (Younger, Usher and McEwan) and up to half a dozen full or part-time nurses covering essential shifts. If you were awake in the night, you might see a dark figure, distinguished by creaking shoes, passing by your bed. This was the elderly Sister Simpson on permanent night-duty.

She has stuck in my mind as an unsolved mystery. To opt for permanent night-duty seemed like choosing death over life. Now, with most of life's vagaries laid bare, I can think of a few good reasons for her choice, none of them really pleasant. She did not look like a criminal hiding from the police. Could she have been leading two lives, one during daylight hours and one on the nightshift? Maybe she had a dependent to look after and was busy night and day. She was an elderly woman and I felt there must have been some extraordinary explanation for her unusual choice.

During my stay there was one nocturnal incident that I missed entirely by sleeping through the whole thing. We had a visit from a *man* in our strictly female preserve sometime after midnight – around 2 a.m. I was told the next day. The ward was quickly roused and all those awake watched as he proceeded to do a round in the best medical fashion, asking each patient if they were satisfied with their treatment or had anything to complain of.

The intruder seemed amiable and was, in fact, a lawyer on his way home from what must have been a lively dinner in the city judging by the amount he had drunk. It was the subject of ribald jokes for the next few weeks. One of the male patients said he'd heard that the entire population of the ward was piled on top of the poor man trying to stake a claim.

Our invader, at least, seemed to be driven either by curiosity or goodwill. Maybe, made bold by his intake of alcohol, he just wanted to visit his investment.

I have heard since of another visitation at a sister sanatorium, the *Cheshire Joint* in Loggerheads, but this one was quite differently motivated. The matron had arrived in one of the women's wards to take the morning roll-call which involved a simple head count. But this morning, however many times she counted, she got the full count plus one. When, finally, she decided to check each of the beds, she found a tramp asleep in the end one. A cold night, easy access and an empty bed had been too much for him to resist.

It is remarkable that neither of these incidents seems to have generated fright of any kind, just intense curiosity and amusement. Boredom is a great aid to serenity. We live in a different world now.

I was sorry to miss the excitement of the lawyer's visit but it woke me to a new awareness of my situation. When I wondered how he had got into the grounds, I was told the gates were never shut. He had only to walk through them. Since the hospital entrance was not in my line of bed-bound vision, I had no knowledge of this open access. My life had shrunk to the point where the entrance or exit was as invisible and as unattainable as Timbuctoo.

'Oh,' I said, puzzled, 'and yet they have all that broken glass on top of the walls. It's just like diamonds in this sun.' It did not seem logical with an unguarded gateway.

Maisie gave me an old-fashioned look. 'To keep the men in,' she said. 'To stop them legging it over the wall and going home when nobody's looking.'

I pondered for a few moments stupidly on whether men were more home-loving than women or maybe just more adventurous.

1950-51 was not a time of overt sexual awareness. *Tropic of Cancer* by Henry Miller was still banned, as was Lawrence's novel, *Lady Chatterley's Lover*. It would be several more years before Nabokov's *Lolita* was published and decades before it was seen on film. No one was yet bold enough to produce books or films exploring sexuality. Only a few years previously, four friends and I in our school-leaving class had been wondering about the process of childbirth. We would more than likely be involved in it at some time in the future, after all. Three of us, seventeen-year-old girls, hazarded opinions as to how it happened and we were all wrong.

But, of course, the real shock was the realisation that the outside world was being protected from the patients rather than the other way round. We assented of course in keeping our infection to ourselves, but it is one thing to volunteer and another to be constrained, however kindly the constraint is applied.

From 1911, when care and control of tuberculosis had been handed over to the local authorities, the number of sanatoria had multiplied, but even with this extra care the most that could be hoped for was to slow down the progress of the disease. It was an uncertain and long-term process and in the early years of the twentieth century there was much resentment at the cold and comfortless surroundings and the repressive treatment then practised. But we in the Royal Victoria in 1950 had the luxury of knowing that efforts at finding a cure were proceeding in several different directions and all were being properly monitored. There was a new energy and determination at work.

Even during my time on the ward, treatment for TB was gradually shifting away from surgery, the most promising treatment on offer, towards chemotherapy. My ward combined the two approaches. It included at least one lobectomy case (where an entire lobe of the lung is removed to get rid of the focus of infection), one resection (where a piece of lung is removed) and two thoracoplasty cases (where a section of each rib is removed from the patient's back in a straight line to permit the lung below to be crushed.)

Many years later I heard from a fellow-sufferer treated in Ireland that the hollows left by the crushed or missing lung were filled up with table-tennis balls in an attempt to maintain symmetry for the patient. Otherwise the flesh would sink into a massive hollow at the site of the operation. I planned a blackly comic detective story where a corpse, intended to sink, stuck bizarrely out of the water on one side and quickly brought the murderer to justice.

All of these major surgery cases were furnished with a long mirror at the foot of the bed, a strangely luxurious detail in our Spartan surroundings, so that the patient could correct any tendency to sag or lean on their affected side. I can understand the need for this, but wonder whether it (or some equivalent) should have been extended to pneumothorax patients. This lesser procedure in my case was on my right side and I was surprised to be told recently by a physiotherapist that I have a dropped right shoulder. A couple of years with a deflated lung may have been the reason, but possibly it was caused by all the books I have carried over the years.

These last operations were all designed not to rest the lung temporarily, but to put it permanently out of action. The patient would then have to rely on whatever area of lung remained in order to breathe.

The treatment of collapsing the lung was not confined to the under-arm region. We referred glibly to being a RAP (right artificial pneumothorax), a LAP (left artificial pneumothorax) or a PP (pneumo-peritoneum.) In the last case, air-pressure to shrink the lung was applied to the area below the ribs and left the recipient, whether male or female, appearing to be in an interesting condition. Five to six months pregnant was the general consensus, although the word pregnant was not used. Favoured terms were *expecting* or, more insultingly, *gone*.

Incredibly some patients functioned with both right and left pneumothoraxes and a pneumo-peritoneum in place and must have had very limited room for air within the lung. We were often reminded:

Never run if you can walk,
Walk, if you can stand,
Stand, if you can sit,
Sit, if you can lie.

This did not need repeating in their case. Inevitably we all added our own last line:

Never breathe if you can help it!

I used to wonder anxiously whether the young women who were singled out for treatment with a pneumo-peritoneum would look permanently pregnant in their recovery and what this would do to their reputations and/or their marriage prospects.

The crushing of the phrenic nerve, just below the neck on either side, brought about a virtual pneumothorax (collapsed lung) at diaphragm level that was more permanent than a PP.

All of the pneumothorax operations could dislodge organs like the heart and reposition them elsewhere. There were at least two patients I knew in the Royal Victoria whose hearts had deviated towards the wrong side. It filled me with awe that your heart could go wandering, apparently without dire consequences. There was at this time current on the wards of the Cheshire Joint sanatorium a parody of *My Heart's in the Highlands.*

My heart's in the mattress,
My heart is not here
I endeavour to locate it,
But it's gone away I fear.

In addition the phrenic crush could affect facial muscles from time to time.

Joan is the girl with the half-closed eye,
caused by the phrenic crush.
She takes the winks of passers-by
and doesn't even blush.

Taking all this into account, I hold myself lucky to have got off with a simple RAP. None of these surgical treatments was free of risk, but they did frequently revive the health of seriously ill patients. Without the surgical procedures to close cavities in the lung and so prevent the spread of the bacillus, a steady 80% of sufferers in the first half of the twentieth century died within five years.

When I embarked on this memoir, I did not realise how absolutely on the cusp of change my own illness was. I developed TB at one of the most significant points in its entire medical history. Up to the point when I became ill, all the drugs that had been tried over the centuries had either been proved ineffectual or had to be abandoned as too toxic for the human body. The TB bacterium, that can withstand almost boiling water, is a tough organism.

Before my diagnosis and treatment, surgery was being used as the only aid to survival, but during the fifties there was a gradual, sustained and increasing movement away from surgery in favour of the drugs that were on trial. Streptomycin and PAS were the first to be successful. However, in spite of this potent magic, I was to have one more brush with the knife before real progress was made in my treatment.

Setbacks, spreading temporary gloom, were not unusual. Often, when a fellow patient left our orbit, we would ask where she had disappeared to and were told 'Southfield'. Oh, I would think, progress at last. But they were never heard of again. They stayed alive in our memories, a kind of ghost. I learned to be wary of the name of Southfield. Whether it *was* a convenient fiction for awkward questions, as I suspected, I never managed to verify. It would have been a neat way of avoiding giving a patient a demoralising answer. Southfield Sanatorium was a reality, I knew, and it may have been used as a progression towards cure, but, strangely, neither I nor a very organized friend was later able to find it. It was an elusive place.

I imagine it was the fear of having to cope with major surgery of some kind rather than innate delicacy that kept us from asking too many questions, otherwise boredom would have ensured that we knew every detail. What we did know at the time was that, in the case of thoracoplasty operations, a general anaesthetic was not always suitable and this meant that the still-conscious patient could hear pieces of his or her own ribs being thrown into an enamel bucket under the operating table.

You might think that such horror stories would lead to despair but in a disastrous situation you cannot allow yourself to give way. You can hope that something like this will never happen to you, but if it does you will look it in the eye and thank whoever discovered our potent local anaesthetics.

When I was discussing this with one of the other patients who had undergone major surgery, she said, 'Oh, but we had the music.' This was the first time I had heard of music being played during surgery; an inspiration, whether to pace the surgeon or distract the patient. It had not, however, distracted me entirely a couple of days earlier, when Dr. McPherson had been singing *'The Lark in the Clear Air'* during my air-pressure refill. I felt extra pressure on each down beat and on the high notes:

*...as I **hear** the swee-eet **la-ark** sing*
*I-in the **clea-ear** air of the **day-ay**.*

We may indeed have heard the sweet lark sing. The grounds were alive with birdsong in summer and the singers were our constant visitors. Windows surrounded the lozenge-shaped wards on three sides allowing them to flit in and out all day long, provided there was nothing to disturb them. They never interrupted doctor's rounds or mealtimes when there were people hurrying about, but they had learned that the ones in the beds were no threat and came to steal our fruit. Like our visitors, they enjoyed grapes best and since these were still in very short supply, it was often a race between patient and marauders.

Sometimes they would fly up in panic at the unexpected entrance of a nurse and blunder into the part of the window that remained unopened. If they were merely concussed, we nursed them in cupped hands until they were strong enough to fly away. If their necks were broken, a frisson of mourning ran round the ward. It was quickly suppressed on the *'only-a-bird'* scale of values, but there was a recognition that the birds were waging, like all creation, a battle for survival and that this pathetic handful had lost out in the struggle. We liked the birds. They reminded us of the world outside.

It was during my stay in the Royal that I discovered I was a tree-hugger. The term was not widely used then to suggest contempt as it now does and I had developed an overpowering obsession with the trees outside my window. The form it took was a need for physical contact. I wanted above everything else to put my arms round the massive girth of the straightest and tallest tree and believed that it would energise me and speed my recovery. This belief in the healing power of nature which my mother certainly endorsed may have been pure instinct, but it was no doubt reinforced by the virtual Eden of my earliest years.

I was born during the great depression and my father had left the regular army at a time of mass unemployment. He was lucky to have landed his clerical job in the Parks Department, which entitled him to the tenancy of one of a row of estate workers' cottages with gardens at the front and privies at the end of the gardens. It was a thick-walled, stone building on what had been a country estate, although by that time it was well within the expanding bounds of Edinburgh. The estate of Saughton Hall had been taken over as a public park but had kept most of the features of its grace-and-favour past.

We lived cheek by jowl with the gardener on one side and the farrier on the other. Sometimes a horse would be brought along the cobbles in front of the cottages and we would have the thrill of riding on its massive back. Horses still played a big part in our daily lives, even in a large town. Our daily milk was delivered from a horse and cart driven by a young woman with rosy cheeks. The cart was a jaunting carriage.

It must have been a hard and inconvenient life for my mother. The only source of water (cold) was a tap outside and every drop had to be carried in and heated on a small range, whether for washing, laundry, or cooking.

For us children, however, it was quite a different matter. We were a stone's throw from the Water of Leith, the river that ran from the west through Longstone where my mother lived as a child, down through the beautiful Dean Village in the heart of Edinburgh and on into the Firth of Forth. At the point where it flowed through Saughton Park it became a broad burn, where we fished for minnows, and I never tired of watching the swans at the foot of a miniature waterfall by the Band Stand.

One potent memory is of a trip to Edinburgh Zoo with my father. He decided to walk us home rather than take the bus and we came back through the grounds of Saughton Hall. It had been a long trek with my young sister begging 'Up!' to be carried every few minutes. We had all grown silent. We passed the rose garden with its little love knots of box hedging, the sun-dial which read *Mark but the hours of sunshine!* and the empty manor house, its mellow stone beautiful in the setting sun. As we came abreast of the flag-pole over the door, we caught sight of an owl sitting on the spar, blinking from its hunched feathers. It was a magical moment and the combination of wildness and peace made it an image that has lasted ever since. We started smiling. Nearly home.

Maybe the trees at the Royal Victoria gave me a subconscious desire to be back there in that first place that I called home. Who knows? I was too wary of the general desire to make fun of things in a dull world to make my tree-hugging instincts public. I kept them to myself.

In spite of the inevitable uncertainties in our march towards health, we found surprising splashes of colour in our arrested lives. One day I fell into a deep sleep and woke to see a startlingly bright exotic-looking bird flying past the window.

'What's that beautiful bird with the flashing colours?' I asked. 'I haven't seen it before.'

'What colour is it?' someone asked.

'Blue and green.'

'Escaped budgie,' said Maisie, without looking up.

Stupid of me, I thought. We'd had one at home for about four years in the war. Jockie, who became Mary, when he laid an egg.

CHAPTER 6
Baggage

Mary, the budgie, was another casualty of the war. As it progressed and goods became scarcer and scarcer, we could no longer get the seed that she needed and we soon noticed that she had lost her verve and her beak was discoloured. Perhaps it says much about the times that we did not consider getting her to a vet. All our efforts had become the war effort. The vets were probably at the front and so was the money.

We tried the few alternative foods available, including bread-crumbs, and when, later, she started convulsing, we brought her round with medicinal compound (brandy) several times. Inevitably, however, we found her one morning dead on her back with her little twiggy claws in the air.

This sudden resurrection in memory, set against the appearance of the exotic escapee and my failure to connect the two, made me realise how a different setting can change things. If my caged domestic pet could become this sizzling emblem of liberty, what might this new setting do for the problems we all carry around with us?

None of us had arrived at the Royal Victoria without emotional baggage and I knew already of several sad situations left behind in the old world – grievous losses, estrangements, problems that seemed insoluble. One very sad case, although it was recounted in a matter-of-fact way as a not particularly interesting fact of life, involved a recently acquired friend, John Levey.

John and I met at one of our weekly air-refill sessions. He was slightly built and had dark, lustrous eyes, a scintillating wit and – let's not beat about the bush – a very large nose. He was the only other student in the sanatorium and this may have effected some gravitational pull between us. At any rate I became the focus of his attention. He lived in one of the open-ended chalets in a nicely wooded part of the grounds and was always inciting me to go back to my ward via the woods, although unsupervised meetings of the sexes were frowned on.

During one of these diversions he told me a little of his family history in a humorous attempt to explain his very large nose. When he told me that he was of mixed Jewish parentage, he stepped into my heart. Not that I am Jewish, but we all knew what the Jews had been through in Belsen, Dachau, Auschwitz and other concentration camps of shameful memory. We knew that in Nazi Germany Jews had been destined for genocide, the so-called final solution, and we were desperate to make restitution in whatever way we could.

He told me that he had had an elder brother with consumption whose kidneys were affected. He had donated one of his own kidneys to his invalid brother, then became consumptive himself. John was thus in double jeopardy. His brother died.

Then there were the two mothers who had each left three small children at home. Anna, one of the mothers, was in the bed next to mine and worried that by the time she was sent home the children would have become attached to another carer whom they perhaps regarded as their mother. Anna was very protective by nature, pre-empting disagreements on the ward almost before they began and laying a tactful hand on every situation. She was a natural mother, but parents with TB were not normally allowed to see their children. Would Anna even be recognized when she finally saw hers? As a mother she was suffering a triple bereavement.

We did not talk about these things unless they emerged incidentally in the course of conversation. People stepped daily over yawning fissures of concern, pretending they were not there. But, treatment aside, the enforced absence from life's stresses could have a beneficial effect. It gave us a rest and time to regroup our forces. It prolonged the life that had come under threat. In my case I was all too aware that I'd been given a chance to float for a while, to forget what had become a painful and insoluble problem. No-one else knew of it and I didn't intend that anyone should. I tried not to know it myself when it surfaced, but a careless word from Betty Shiels brought the dark cloud of knowing back across the horizon. My heaviest baggage. And it was about to fall on me.

In general we enjoyed our bonus playtime but sometimes it palled. This dull afternoon was one of those tedious times. We had been having a casual talk about films and someone asked me who my favourite film star was. I stalled. Was it Cary Grant, the smooth, groomed master of comedy? Or Gregory Peck, the tall, saturnine, reluctant hero? Or James Stewart, the corn-reared legal eagle? I stalled a moment too long.

'Don't ask *her* about films,' said Betty. 'She's too wrapped up in books.' Then nastily, 'We can't *all* be students you know.'

Until that moment I had not been aware that being a student could be considered an offence, but the hostility in the words brought the game to an early close and left me to my thoughts about student life and the Black Douglas. I called him that because he terrified me, as the original in Scottish history must have terrified his victims.

The Black Douglas was my tutor in English literature.

Starry-eyed as I was, following my parents' reverence for education, I had expected from this professional relationship nothing but help and encouragement – even praise maybe. After all, the function of tutoring is a protective and pastoral one.

As far as my grasp of English went I was in a very privileged position. I had spent half my life reading. It was an absorbing passion and I loved words and their nuances. Far more powerful than numbers with their rigid values, words shifted and blended according to the context. They were alive.

I had never been beaten in an English exam since the age of seven when Jessie Smith asked me in a whisper the meaning of *'conspiracy'*.

'You put *'plot,'* I whispered back. 'I'll put *'plan.'*

It was one conspiracy that misfired. She got one mark for *'plot'*: I got half a mark for *'plan'*. She beat me in the test by half a mark.

Big-headed? Well, maybe I was. I had left a large school as the undisputed champion in my favourite subject and with First Prizes in two key areas of study, English and Modern Languages. There were plenty of subjects where I was miles away from being a champion of any kind. In any case I was always aware, as my mother insisted, that talent in any walk of life is a gift, a privilege. You have a duty to nourish it .

Now here I was, a university student studying literature, nourishing my gift like mad, and it seemed to be all for nothing.

My tutorial group was a bit unbalanced; ten ex-servicemen and Meriel and me. To me the men were all heroes. My father, as a former regular soldier, had been called up a month before the war started and was absent for seven formative years of my life. All my concentration had been trained on the war effort. Only when the war was over would life – real life – resume. I was there in spirit on the far-off fields of conflict. I was naive enough to imagine that all survivors would meet in a spirit of friendship and go forward together into the new age which would be a better one than that we had just lived through. This group of men, however, was a very silent, withheld one, unexpectedly so.

Meriel, to do her justice, did try to open a dialogue with me, but all her conversations were about clothes, an odd subject in a country still strait-jacketed by post-war austerity. Since she was talking to someone still wearing a school Burberry for want of any other coat to wear, the chats went nowhere.

After a few weeks Meriel disappeared, perhaps to another tutorial group. I wish that I had done the same, but I didn't know then that you could and, even if I had known, I was at that time too scrupulous to do it.

With the ex-servicemen I was too shy to make any moves towards acquaintance. Their presence in the tutorial group was largely part of the post-war move towards a more equal society following the Labour landslide victory of 1945. I seem to remember a few fleeting smiles from one or two of the men and that was it. To be so ignored was unusual. School Burberry or no, in every other group I was used to a more flattering degree of attention.

But then they did not talk to one another either and any sign of animation died on the stroke of ten with the entry of the Black Douglas. From then on the men sat staring ahead with fixed expressions, sometimes with arms folded, while our tutor tried to open a dialogue. We were less aware of body language in those days, but even I could see that barriers had been erected. Looking back I am aware of a remarkable level of guardedness.

In the tutorial were a fair-haired Yorkshireman with slightly protruding blue eyes, a more polished English veteran whose prospective father-in-law was someone in the public eye (he went on to become a noted English scholar himself), a dark-headed likable highlander whose first language was Gaelic, and another, larger-framed highlander with a Viking name. Then there was a dapper Englishman called Eric (another Viking name) who became quite a well-known television producer. The others, as far as my memory goes, are history.

Our tutor tried in the wrong direction, I think. When his first tentative questions were met with silence, he simplified them to a fairly moronic level, adding insult to injury and

68

possibly injuring himself too. It must have been discouraging for him to know that no dialogue was taking place, even at this very low level. The rapid delivery of his questions, as he sat ramrod straight in front of us, coupled with nervous fits and starts, suggested less than complete confidence, which must have dwindled further as time went on. I found out much later that English Literature was not his subject. In my particular tutorial, we were sold seriously short.

It was the war situation again still distorting things years after its close. It was not my first encounter with an unorthodox teacher. Manpower had been and still was abnormally low. At senior school in the fifth and sixth years we had had a disabled veteran for maths, Major Balfour; a lovable man, but stone deaf.

'Sir, is the homework to be in ink?'

'Open the window by all means, m'boy! It *is* a bit stuffy.'

A timid hand in the air. 'Please for leave, Sir?'

'Certainly, m'dear, the graph paper's on the front desk.'

We loved him but had limited success in the maths exam because of the complete lack of communication. Although as the top A-stream class we were all expected to pass, only a third of us did.

Some of these men sitting before the Black Douglas would have been through hell simply surviving the war. My own uncle Will had gone down with *HMS Laforey* in the action at Anzio. I later read a description of the scene as the ship went down. It was utter confusion on board what with the screeching of shells and the screaming of men. The sea was hazardous with oil leaked from the submerging ship and dotted with the heads of would-be survivors, most of whom never made it to land or any other rescue. The awful finality of the loss of ship and hundreds of men in a mere three and a half minutes was shocking.

These men sitting in a circle with me would perhaps already have seen too much of life – and death – to welcome an introduction to it, albeit through literature, from someone who had not walked the same paths. At least this might be the explanation of their unreceptive attitude.

I began to notice that my own remarks and attempts to contribute were not welcomed by my tutor. I tried to stay silent but it was so embarrassing and unnecessary, painful even, that in the end I would make a timid offering. Sometimes it was ignored. Sometimes it was taken up and a discussion of sorts developed.

It was in the monthly Rhetoric tests that I came officially unstuck. These were tests on the virtues of Unity, Coherence and Proper Emphasis in the stylistic areas of literature. Although administered over the whole year by a senior lecturer, our papers were marked by our own tutors. Marks were out of 50 and I was puzzled and disappointed to find my first paper had netted only 28 marks, 56%. In geography I would have *deserved* 56%; I was rubbish at geography, being generally spooked by maps. As a fairly small child I had sat through an interminable lesson on contours (aka hills and valleys) peering at a pink and red *road* map of the British Isles. I looked in vain for the Southern Uplands, the Cheviot Hills, the Ochils, the Moorfoots, and MacGillycuddy's Reeks. I later spent a few happy years teaching amongst the gentle Moorfoots, but still do not know where to find MacGillycuddy's Reeks. I think they are in Eire. Geography has remained a nearly closed book.

In English I was used to 83% - 85%. What on earth had I done wrong? Misunderstood one of the questions? I re-read them all but could not find a lead. Maybe this particular paper was always marked very severely? I asked the half-dozen girls I'd been at school with who were taking the same tests. We had been in the same class at Boroughmuir so I knew the relative pecking order. Their marks varied between 76% and 90%. None had anything as low as my own 56%. It did not make sense however hard I tried. None of the scores in my own group had been made public; we all sat in a ring, unspeaking, with our papers in front of us, pretending indifference. No-one else gave any sign that their marks were unexpected or surprising. And shame kept me silent. There was little or no discussion on what was, after all, a very simple exercise. There were no comments on my paper to reveal where I had fallen short. I would have to keep an eye on this.

And everything else, as it turned out. The monthly rhetoric marks remained low, but so did all the work set and marked by the Black Douglas. In a paper on 'Books and Writers of Your Generation' I homed in on H.G. Wells, G.B. Shaw, Aldous Huxley, Somerset Maugham – some of the latest to be filtered through the literary percolator. Although their lives overlapped substantially with my own, the scarlet comments on my essay were no fewer. *'Is this your generation? How old are you?'* I was eighteen. It was to be another seven years before Francoise Sagan hit the bookshelves at the age of eighteen with *Bonjour Tristesse.*

I never found out why he set such an essay subject. I was already saying hello to tristesse with each returned piece of work.

One of the rhetoric tests had invited us to correct stylistic errors in passages from three well-known authors' work. In two cases the faults were self-evident; the third seemed without flaw. However the question did stipulate three, so I transposed two brief phrases where the position seemed unimportant. The change made absolutely no difference to the meaning. This time I was held up to ridicule by an outburst unexpected in an adult situation. 'Here is a girl who thinks she can improve upon Sir Walter Scott!' I waited to be hauled out and slippered. It was a severe humiliation to someone who had shouldered wartime responsibilities and who felt too mature for such treatment.

The most bizarre episode was in the instructions he gave us for writing an essay on the poet Alexander Pope. He told us at least three times to be sure to illustrate Pope's *scurrility*, looking round the group to make sure we had all heard. I imagined that his gaze lingered longer on me but by that time I was also imagining a gleam of enjoyment at my discomfiture every time he gave my work back

The dictionary gives *scurrilous* the meaning 'grossly or obscenely abusive' so it seemed an odd requirement. I knew that

Pope had a spiteful side but the couplets that I had so far encountered seemed funny rather than offensive. This one, aimed at the throne, for instance:

> *Here Thou, Great Anna, whom three Realms obey,*
> *dost sometimes Counsel take and sometimes Tay (tea)*

That was never going to bring down the monarchy. It sounded more like literary flirtation.

I went to the library and found a book on Pope by Edith Sitwell and finally picked out a quote illustrating scurrility.

One of Pope's good friends was Lady Mary Wortley Montague, a much-travelled and learned woman remembered by most of us for introducing a vaccine (actually cowpox) from Europe into Britain to combat the ravages of smallpox. She even gave the vaccine to her beloved son to lessen public fear of the illness, which was a killer as terrifying in its day as consumption.

No one seems to know why Pope had it in for Lady Mary, who was a socialite, living largely apart from her husband, but she is here in this couplet, thinly disguised as Sappho, the Lesbian poet of classical times.

> *From furious Sappho scarce a milder fate,*
> *Pox'd by her love or libell'd by her hate.*

The accusation of sexual licence alleging syphilis was outrageous and the veiled reference to Lady Mary's shortcomings as a mother quite unjustified.

Well, I thought, I've done as he said, although it went against the grain, so I was wholly unprepared for the remarks in the margin of my essay when he gave it back. He had written, *I hope you do not know the meaning of this. I hope **your sin** is ignorance.*

This time I was in no doubt that he took pleasure in seeing how I received his sallies and was even smiling at me in a challenging way, head cocked on one side, eyes glinting with malice. I sat with flaming cheeks for a few minutes before leaving. He had now indicted me for incompetence, stupidity, arrogance and impropriety or worse. It was more than time to call a halt but I didn't know what to do. I was the first of my family to attend university and had no knowledge of how to proceed.

Who was the higher power to appeal to, if there was one? I had been brought up to believe that professional standards, especially in a university, were above reproach. He, the Black Douglas, was the person appointed to guide my footsteps, not paralyse them. He was the person I was supposed to go to with problems and complaints.

Literature was a subject where my ambition rose above a mere pass. I did not want this poor first impression to influence any later assessments. It was my future that he was handling so roughly.

In all this sorry story there had been a brighter side. The other area of English Studies, English Language, carried equal marks in any assessments and in this there was no problem. Certificates of Merit and Distinction fell comfortingly around me, but I did not want to pursue it, if it meant spending my life correcting the punctuation of the unwary or tracing words back to their roots in Primitive Germanic.

There had been one other small, sanity-saving incident. My second-year literature exam paper was not marked by the B.D., but a young woman new to me. My marks immediately ballooned and instead of carping and unfair criticism I had flattering comments like 'An excellent paper! You should do more of this!'

By the time the rogue x-ray hurried me into the Royal Victoria I was clinging to this knowledge as salvage from the wreckage of my hopes and wondering how to escape the clutches of a sadist. The call to this other rendezvous had not been as totally unwelcome as it should have been. I had come up against a hostility that was unexpected, unaccountable, and menacing; something for which I was in no way equipped.

CHAPTER 7
The Smyler with the Knyf under his Cloke

One significant difference between patient care in 1951 and now is that patients today are kept informed about their treatment and any decision to change it. Halfway through the twentieth century there seemed to be no obligation to give the patient anything more than the basic facts about an illness and so, in the Royal Victoria, I was constantly relying on the longer-stay patients to fill in the gaps in my understanding of various situations.

When one day I was told I was being sent to a nearby general hospital for adhesions section, all I could elicit from the ward sister was that my lung was reflating itself too quickly because of adhesions and needed to be rested more completely. Normally a collapsed lung would absorb the air put into the pleural cavity in about a week, requiring refills at that point; mine needed to be done twice a week.

Maisie added a comment or two after Sister had gone, suggesting that everybody had adhesions (fibrous tissues between lung and chest wall resulting from previous infections) and that my lung was too healthy to do as it was told and stay down. This was an appealing idea and kept me buoyed up through the critical manoeuvre and beyond it. In reality the situation was far from denoting a healthy lung; this was Maisie's way of being supportive. As a patient who had recently had a resection, she had already experienced most of the problems that novice patients like myself were grappling with and regularly presented what was frightening in a constructive light. She was a valuable friend.

On the whole I may have had no more than an average number of chest infections, but I do remember suffering severe pain a couple of years earlier which had turned out to be an attack of pleurisy. After taking the word pleurisy back to its root, a worthwhile pastime for the student of language (according to our language professor), I quipped to my sister that my lung was weeping – stylishly – in French. Perhaps the pleurisy had caused the adhesions.

No one looks forward to an operation but, thanks to Maisie, I saw this piece of surgery as a minor hurdle and have only recently become aware that it was, at one time, feared as much as a thoracoplasty because of the danger of post-operative infection.

The thought of the pending operation was grim, but without it I would not so soon have met Isla Jamieson who was my fellow-patient on the hospital trip and soon to be my ward-mate.

Isla was an arresting girl to look at with jet-black hair, cut short and bushy. Her colour was naturally high. This went along with dark eyes and an aquiline nose. She was tallish and slim. Most of us were slim. Although she could be quite animated in conversation there was a stillness in her demeanour that seemed to invite confidences.

Our journey by ambulance to the nearby hospital took only a few minutes but even that short time was enough to release a stream of pent-up thoughts from each of us. What she had to tell about how she came to be in the Victoria was the stuff of high drama.

In the long-ago past, which was actually only a few months previously, she had lived happily at home with her father, mother, and sister, Myrna. It happened that Isla's best friend, Margaret, had a boy-friend who was a medical student studying TB and what he had learned made him apprehensive enough to decide that he and she should both be x-rayed. Margaret was too nervous to go to the hospital alone and asked Isla to keep her company and to be x-rayed at the same time. Isla innocently agreed, then the two of them waited with bated breath for the result. Margaret's chest, as it turned out, was clear, but Isla did have a patch on one lung.

This was bad news and the rest of the Jamieson family were lined up to be x-rayed in turn. This time it was an almost complete rout. Her sister Myrna had a shadow on one lung, and Mr Jamieson was found to have a tumour in his lung so advanced that nothing could be done to remove it. He was advised to give up work and do the things he enjoyed doing.

Poor Mrs Jamieson, I thought, seeing her family fall around her. She must be under an unbearable amount of stress and fear.

'What about Myrna?' I asked.

'Well, she's still having treatment, but she's greatly improved,' Isla said with obvious relief.

'That's wonderful!' I said. 'What about your dad? Is he going downhill fast?'

'No, it's incredible. They x-rayed him a few weeks ago and the tumour's shrunk to vanishing point. They almost failed to find it.'

This was an audacious answer. Consumption and cancer were never mentioned without mentally crossing the fingers. Even today cancer will be referred to as 'The Big C' in a superstitious attempt to deflect lightning.

'You're joking,' I said.

'No. Now would I?' she answered soberly. 'They couldn't see it on the x-ray. Apparently this sort of thing's been known to happen in the past, but very rarely.'

This breathtaking reprieve, like a sword-blade lifted from a bare neck, seemed to me almost like a mark of divine favour, so that when I later met her parents on their visits, it was always with great pleasure. To me they had become legendary. I imagined all of them with the glowing, haloed outline of the modern breakfast cereal ads.

However on that day Isla and I had more immediate things to worry about. We were put through a series of x-rays, blood tests and a lung-function test. I remember most clearly being surprised that the young woman doctor seemed equally delighted by the lung-function test results of each of us in turn, even though mine registered one third less on the dial than Isla's.

Later in the evening we were told that Isla's operation would take place the next morning. I was to have a bronchoscopy. The word was familiar enough, but otherwise my ignorance was profound. They gave me no reason for the change of plan.

By the time I was ready to have my bronchi examined, Isla had gone back to the Victoria and I was lying on a trolley in an empty room beside a tray of instruments. Every one was very long, very bright and shiny and, above all, very straight. These can't be for me, I thought, I'm not that shape, but then a youngish doctor appeared and his eye swept over them. Even then I expected to see a second figure appear behind him, flexing a softer instrument of some kind. I was still looking over his shoulder when a voice said, 'Open wide!'

Thank goodness, I thought, as he sprayed the back of my throat with something cold. I'll soon be asleep. But nothing happened. I remained wide awake. Only my throat grew numb and unresponsive. I can't breathe, my mind registered, and I instinctively put my hands up to ward off his approach. He had the nearest rod in his hand. It looked about 18" long.

'Lie still!' he barked. 'There's an enormous space down there for breathing. You're fine.' His confidence did not transmit itself to me. If your throat is paralysed, you are certainly not conscious of breathing.

I managed to relax marginally. At least he had understood the problem even though I don't think I had actually uttered the words.

Best to draw a veil over the next few minutes. I was afraid of choking or coughing as the instruments were inserted. A considerable time later, which might only have been a fraction of a minute, someone said, 'I can't find her fourth dorsal vertebra,' and I wondered whether this was temporary or permanent – and what they wanted it for. At any rate I followed my fourth dorsal vertebra down into a black hole until the inspection was over. I was finally left alone on my trolley until a nurse came to wheel me back to the side ward that Isla and I had shared.

The experience was frightening and stressful and when I afterwards brought up some blood, I felt that there were questions to be asked.

Bronchoscopy is used as sparingly as possible when it is necessary to look closely at a specific area of the bronchi in more detail than an x-ray permits. We naturally wanted to know what results the examination had revealed and my mother agreed to ask the questions. As a former nurse she spoke at least some of the language, but she could not get through the obfuscation barrier and was put off with vague terms like 'nothing to worry about', 'simple procedure' and 'not dangerous'. When she asked directly why it had been necessary, the doctor answered, 'To widen her tubes; they are very narrow.'

This most likely accounted for the blood, but some kind of anaesthetic would have been kinder, as would the use of the flexible bronchoscope (which at that time had not been invented). Even more useful would have been some kind of description of the procedure and explanation for it before it was carried out.

A look at the use of the bronchoscope nowadays shows that the patient is given anti-anxiety medication and sedatives like morphine before the operation, is monitored for heart and blood-pressure deviation during the event, and monitored afterwards at 15-minute intervals until the gag reflex is restored, proving that the throat is no longer paralysed. From my limited experience I would say that all are necessary. In 1950 there was a 1% mortality rate from this avowedly 'not dangerous' procedure, as well as the possibility of a heart attack or kidney damage. At the very least the patient could end up with broken teeth.

The real object of my visit was still pending and, despite the lateness of the hour, I was wheeled down a long, deserted, hospital corridor with dim, wartime lighting the following evening. Pools of dim light from the lamps on the walls gave way to repeated pools of shadow and the polished linoleum reflected this in a watery light that seemed to flow along as the trolley did.

The experience was quite surreal mainly because the male porter wore make-up and a bright, gauzy, chiffon scarf. His high-octane red lipstick threw into greater contrast the grey-white tones of his angular face and the interruptions of five-o'clock stubble on his chin.

At this time in my life I knew nothing of homo-eroticism or any other gender deviation and was totally unprepared for the encounter. I felt aggrieved. Surely they could have given me a proper nurse.

Maybe I felt nervous because I had been warned that they needed me to remain conscious during the operation. They needed to monitor my reactions for a successful outcome. It had made me feel isolated, like a pioneer explorer expected to report back from the interior and not at all sure what I would encounter or how I would get back. I needed support.

Proper nurse my porter may not have been, but proper human being he most certainly was. Instead of leaving me once I was on the operating table, he sat down by my head and took my hand in both of his in a reassuring grip. Next he engaged everybody present in light, cheerful conversation. Occasionally he would mutter comments intended only for me. They were low and mainly inaudible, but sounded comfortingly subversive.

Sometimes he would report on the state of my pulse. The fact that it was thin and thready was not surprising. The method of cutting adhesions is to make two small holes, after a local anaesthetic, into the pleural cavity under the arm. Then they introduce a light through one hole and a cauterizing wand through the other and start cutting. The pain was bearable, but the sound of tearing flesh and the smell of its burning, especially when you knew whose flesh it was, were not conducive to a strong, regular pulse.

At last it was over, leaving me extremely grateful to the unnamed porter and respectful to the hospital for supplying a helpful niche to someone who needed it. It seemed to me he had carried the psychological burden of the event. Efficiency could be taken for granted in a large teaching hospital but this porter had added the generous virtue of consideration for the patient. He had provided something other than the instruments of invasion for me to focus on. He had been my human crutch. I was ashamed of my earlier peevishness.

Returning to the Victoria from surgery, I felt frail, battered and lethargic. So much so that I hardly noticed that we had a new doctor on the medical round, until I heard the unfamiliar voice.

'Show me!' he said.

Obediently I raised my arm, disclosing two small, clipped wounds and an area of bruising. There were also a few under-arm hairs that had escaped my feeble attempt to shave after the operation.

'Keep these hairs shaved off!' the face said sternly.

'I wonder what happened to *his,*' I thought. In place of Dr. Mc- Pherson's raven locks there was only a stubble of fair short bristles, the first of the fashionable crew-cuts for men

I wasn't sure I had accurately taken in this unexpected humiliation and waited till the ward door closed before repeating the brusque message to the patients within hearing distance.

'We've all been told,' shouted the others.

'Julie said it was against her religion,' somebody added with a cackle.

Funny about hair, I thought. It's to be kept on here and shaved off there for somebody else's pleasure or convenience. My own mother had been adamant forever that I hang on to my crowning glory. No ear-tip bobs or liberty cuts for me

I was still mildly simmering with resentment in the afternoon, when a rhythmic squeak seemed to herald a very early tea-time and a voice said, 'Would you like us to do anything to your hair?'

I looked from the trolley, laden with lotions, scissors, brushes, combs and shampoo to the two friendly, smiling faces behind it.

'Yes,' I said. 'Cut it off!'

'Cut it off?' they echoed, but seeing that I meant it, they entered into the spirit of the thing. The girls were mobile hairdressers without any headquarters other than their trolley, so the only concession to privacy was the bed-screen which they drew. I gave them carte-blanche so far as style went and simply sat back. It was reckless but that fitted in with my mood.

Snip went the scissors, as one lock after another slithered to the floor. The scissors were laid carefully against first one cheek then the other. They caressed the nape of my neck, crept up the back of my head, lingered lovingly on my brow.

We retired to the bathroom for a shampoo and rinse. A hair-drying session later, ten minutes instead of the usual hour and a half, I fearfully picked up the hand-mirror. Soft wisps of hair shading from light-brown to gold waved across my forehead. Above it on the crown, my heavy, lank hair had gone lyrical. Mild waves lifted and crested from the former glassy sea. Beneath it my face had come suddenly into focus achieving harmony and balance. My nose looked straighter. My mouth lifted at the corners. My ears rested comfortably in crisp, waving hair and two steady eyes looked out on a new world; the one that

I had chosen. Suddenly I felt empowered. It was a feeling that I had not enjoyed for a long time.

The next morning I awaited the consultant's round with only a little latent hostility. He seemed to spend a long time at the other beds and I was lost in my book again before he arrived, only slowly becoming aware of the figure hovering at my side.

Finally I looked up to see two concerned, brown eyes staring into mine.

'That's good,' he said, smiling warmly. 'You look heaps better now.' And he gave my arm an encouraging squeeze as he left the ward.

CHAPTER 8
Life is a gambol: sometimes up, sometimes down

In the ward that I returned to from the General Hospital, I knew virtually no one. I couldn't see why I needed a change of ward, but have since realised that our cases were strictly monitored according to some clearly defined stages on the way to better health. Presumably with my recent surgery behind me I had entered a new category.

It did not do to call this recovery; there were frequent reminders that the condition could not be cured, only arrested. To mark the advances, allowances in mobility were given at each stage. The policy seemed to be an avoidance of stress, whether physical, mental or emotional, so all moves were gradual and smooth.

After the operation I was on Grade 1. This meant that I was no longer on strict bed-rest or tied to the bed-pan round. I could get up and have a leisurely wash or even bathe. If the bath was free of eggs.

In the strict post-war rationing period, eggs were still scarce, but once Eileen made her discovery, relatives brought them in whenever possible. Eileen of the Titian hair, sparkling green eyes and weighty bosom had a background interesting enough in those days to set her on her own little pedestal. She was somebody's mistress; Alfred's to be precise. Alfred was an amiable businessman who looked as if he might have a bowler hat hidden away somewhere. Eileen had a soft Irish voice and was interestingly subversive. She found out that, if you ran the hot tap for ten minutes into an enamel jug with eggs in it, they would be perfectly boiled. This was done under the pretext of taking a bath and my Presbyterian conscience was shocked at the extravagance of this, because the hot water was often allowed to run away, but I was not averse to adding my egg to the pitcher (normally used for rinsing off shampoo after a hair wash). I used to calculate whether it would be possible to have a bath then eat the egg, but decided it would be too cold and unappetising by then. It was such a luxury to be warm that once I was in the water not even a perfectly boiled egg would lure me out.

Why, you might wonder, was it not possible to ask for a pan of water and access to the kitchen? I can only say that, beside the fact that the kitchen was in another building, the regulations left little open to negotiation. In the 1950s, as for many decades before it, medical men were gods, a different breed of creation, and authoritarian with it. Doctors were revered like the Delphic Oracle and nurses were their acolytes. As a result the patient was robbed of all power but the power of assent. It would not have occurred to us to ask if we might boil an egg.

It was to be many years before I discovered that we in The Royal Victoria were a special case, more scrutinised, more recorded, more controlled and more directed than the general patient. Further years were to pass before I knew how, where and why this happened. At the time we heard and, for the most part, we obeyed.

The fact that requests were not encouraged did not prevent the odd attempt to improve things. I was surprised one day to be approached by Dawn Fairfax from my previous ward. She was good company, a slender, vibrant, fair-haired wand of a person. Often, when she spoke, the ward was convulsed with laughter. She told me that she might be sent out to one of the two-bed chalets and asked if I would like to be the one to share with her.

This needed some urgent thought. I was not sure that I was up to being the entire fan club that Dawn's rapier wit deserved. Besides, the chalets did not just have open windows; they had a whole wall missing. When rain or snow was driving in, the groundsmen had to turn them on their massive spindles so that the patients inside faced temporarily in a different direction, away from the weather. In the wards our only concession to the weather was to place our flower vases on the floor against the table struts in case they were blown over in a gale. Their position on the floor gave them a peculiar pathos. Flowers are made to flaunt, to attract attention, not cower in a corner. I thought I should stay with the devil I knew or I might be cowering permanently under the covers, changing the misery of being constantly cold for the misery of being too numb to feel it.

I decided to keep my options open. 'Well,' I said, 'if they asked me to go, I'd go, of course.'

A few days later Dawn moved into a chalet with another live wire, a pretty, dark-haired girl, called Dolores, and all day long the clarion of their laughter rang through the open windows. They seemed to have entered some new, deliriously bright world of their own. It was said they were on happy pills. We did not know at the time how right this was.

Then came a day when a new arrival, two beds away from mine, opened up a whole new range of conversational topics. She was a slight woman with long, brunette hair, swept up and caught at the back of her head. She had an olive complexion and fairly regular features and something set her apart from the rest of the patients. A quiet air of assurance suggested she was used to being heard.

Although there might have been mileage in discussing our illness and its conduct, in reality we almost never did; it would have disclosed too many unpalatable facts. We preferred to coast. That day the newcomer and I covered a massive range of subjects. I think we discussed mainly people and literature and for me it was an exhilarating holiday.

We talked all day across the intervening bed which was hardly fair to the person in it, so I was not wholly surprised when the newcomer asked, during the doctors' round next day, whether she and I could have our beds brought closer together. It was a simple enough request and I stretched my ears for the answer, but it never came. Within the hour she was called out of the ward and never returned.

Presumably these two events were unconnected. Perhaps one of our regular tests for the active stage of the disease had thrown up a positive which would have sent her back to square one in this fateful game of snakes and ladders. Or maybe a bed had become vacant in the mythical Southfield Sanatorium. I never saw her again.

'Who was she?' I asked when it was clear our brief acquaintance was over.

'Oh, Dr. M,' came the answer. 'She lectures at the university.'

Our lives were full of such ships that passed in the night. However, one bit of good luck that came my way was that Isla Jamieson became my neighbour on the other side, so I acquired a soul mate after all. We settled happily into a shared view of life, the universe and everything.

There was a tendency for all of us to lotos-eat. We were like the drugged mariners on Odysseus' voyage back to Ithaca after the Trojan Wars. After eating the mythical lotos plant in the land of the Lotophagi, they forgot their homes and travelled on to Circe's island, where the sorceress enchanted them, making their return home less likely than ever. Something had taken us away from our homeland and something sinister was preventing our return. We relaxed into a state that seemed inevitable, half uncaring and half entranced.

Let us swear an oath and keep it with an equal mind,
In the hollow Lotos-land to live and lie reclined
On the hills like Gods together, careless of mankind.

(Tennyson)

We had not, of course, forgotten life outside the sanatorium, but we remained in a state of suspension. It was a bit like being part of the introduction to a video that keeps replaying because no one has pressed the button to move it on to the next stage.

We made the most of the diversions we had. We still listened to 'Housewife's Choice' and to 'Hospital Requests' and two of the ward's teenagers decided to write a letter of appreciation to a beginner song-writer whose name I have forgotten.

The girls pretended it was strongly tongue-in-cheek and, examining the lyrics, I could see where their reservations were coming from. Every second line of the song began 'With these hands...' and this, although in acknowledged song-writing tradition, came to sound a bit uninventive. I still remember the melody, which, in turn, brings back some of the words:

With these hands I will cling to you
I am yours for ever and a day.

But, although the sentiment was trite to a critical ear, the writer's stock went up with the culmination of the verse:

With these hands I'll provide for you
Should there be a storm at sea, I'll turn the tide for you
And I'll never.... No I'll never... go away.

We all still needed the tide to turn.

The letter had a surprising result. The writers were delighted to have an effusive answer by return of post. It thanked them and said they had saved the song-writer's sanity during a depressing spell when nobody seemed to be listening and the music-market seemed particularly unheeding.

The world had been as insubstantial as a dream; we had no contact with it, but now suddenly, through the ether, it seemed to be a place that we could inhabit again. The letter had something of the thunderclap quality of emailing a complete but celebrated stranger on the opposite side of the world and getting an immediate answer. There *was* something out there.

The girls, the first of a hopefully expanding fan club, kept writing and the lyricist kept producing and improving the songs until he became quite well-known.

We remained becalmed in mid-ocean, however, until one morning I put on my trusty earphones and found them less trusty than usual. Instead of being bombarded with music or voices, I was puzzled by strange creaks, thumps and scratching noises. The thought of doing without my BBC fix was daunting, so in the end I unscrewed the ear-piece on the offending side and out fell an earwig, threatening to validate its name. If it had emerged through one of the volume holes, it would certainly have gone into my ear.

Unfortunately for the troublemaker, I was so appalled to find myself in bed with a creature with so many legs that I gave a start. It fell off the bed and was last seen trundling off with sore feet.

If I had been an old-time seer aboard Odysseus' ship, I would no doubt have predicted that we were about to hear news of some kind and, in a roundabout way, we did.

That same morning the post brought a letter from my friend, Jean, also studying English at Edinburgh University. As I opened it, a newspaper cutting fell out. Scrawled across the top I read, *'Thought you'd be interested in this.'*

No, I wouldn't, I thought sulkily, life is all and only newsprint, and thrust it between two large oranges in my fruit dish while I read the letter. Relenting at coffee time, however, I unfolded it to the small, highlighted passage and read:

ISLANDS UNDER SIEGE
GO WEST, YOUNG MAN! NO LONGER GOOD ADVICE.

The tubercle bacillus, Mycobacterium Tuberculosis, has been fought with every weapon in the medical armoury for centuries and, although never vanquished, its worst ravages have been alleviated in recent years, extending the life of its victims.

However in the islands off the West Coast of Scotland, where the disease has been rife for centuries, the problem is compounded. Islanders are being stricken down at more than the usual rate and infection is currently running at one in three of the population.

Resistance in this isolated population has never been high, but recovery rates are now at vanishing point. Notwithstanding the epic struggles of the war years that may have left the islanders more exposed, epidemiologists fear another factor is at work. They cite the return home of war veterans from the Highland Light Infantry and the Seaforth Highlanders. The men, it is felt, may have imported a strain of the bacillus, to which the depleted highlanders have no resistance whatever.

Things look bleak for our island population, unless the experimental new

90

drug, isoniazid, continues to prove effective. This drug is currently hastening recovery rates in selected hospitals in the Lowlands and the hope is that this lifeline will prove equally effective in The Western Isles, where too many young lives have been spent in isolation from their host communities through this dreadful plague.

A footnote to the article read:

Isonicotinic acid hydrazide is restoring so many endangered lives in recent trials that it is becoming known as "the consumptive's friend". *Early treatments with the drug were so marked by euphoria that the doctors believed they had stumbled on a powerful anti-depressant, but now believe the phenomenon is the simple restoration of well-being to those patients lucky enough to receive it.*

My mind went at once to Dawn and Dolores and the laughter that was still erupting daily from their chalet. They were on new tablets, I knew. They sounded like a woman's name. Was it Ina, as I had thought, or *INAH – isonicotinic acid hydrazide?* Another weapon in the armoury against TB was good news indeed – and this looked like a very good one, a big gun. I felt like cheering.

After digesting the news in the cutting I could see further into the cause of Mary McKenzie's despair. TB was even more of a death sentence in The Western Isles, where Mary had lived, than elsewhere. She had perhaps been brought up throughout her entire life in terror of the blow falling. She had good reason to think, on being diagnosed, that her life was effectively over.

I pondered on the one and only visit from her mother that I had witnessed and the tension we had all felt. Somehow we all knew that Mary was a special case. She had told me, when I broached the subject of the cuttings, that she had staved off the visit by, as she put it, 'telling my mother lies.' She had simply allowed her mother to think that she had been transferred to another hospital as a nurse, not that she was, herself, a patient. She had just left the name of the ward out of the address.

'But why?' I asked.

'My brother, Rory... the TB took him. I thought my mother would have died. I needed to spare her a double loss as long as possible.'

'But Mary, you're still here!' I reminded her.

She merely looked troubled. At last she muttered, 'Oonagh McLeod...'

'She lost her family?'

She nodded. 'Every one. She was never the same again. How she could fill our heads, when she thought our bodies were dying...' Her voice died away to a murmur.

'But, Mary, you will get better,' I encouraged.

'I daren't go home,' she whispered, 'even if......'

'Why not?'

'It is too dangerous for the living.' Her choice of words terrified me. 'We have to live apart – and even then our families are feared as bringers of the death.'

There was a long silence. 'Make your life here then,' I urged. 'The islands have very few jobs to offer anyway; isn't that right?' I could see how living as a pariah would only confirm an expected death sentence.

'It is my home,' she said with dignity.

'Well, visits then, when you're better. This new drug will be the one. You'll see. What did they call it?'

'Ina,' she said uncertainly. I bent over the cutting again and picked out the initials: IsoNicotinic Acid Hydrazide. We were still poring over it, when Sister Lowther arrived to do the weigh-in.

'What's all this, then?' she breezed, seizing the cutting without permission. After a cursory glance she threw it on the desk and turned her attention to me. 'Am I to deduct a pound or half a pound for that orange in your pocket, Bella?'

I squirmed and tried to nudge it into a less obvious position. Filling our dressing-gown pockets with fruit or something heavy to fool the scales had become a tradition. We would only move on to the next grade in mobility when we had proved a weight gain. I was the only patient in the wards around us to have gained no weight whatsoever. Heaving a sigh of resignation I shifted position again for access to my other pocket and produced a small bunch of grapes. They were still in very short supply and I liked them better than oranges. Sister Lowther's eyes lit up and she nodded for me to leave them on the desk, but it didn't spare me the lecture that I had expected.

When Mary had been weighed and left, casting a longing look back at the newsprint on the desk, she turned to me. 'You should know better,' she said, 'than to unsettle people with vague possibilities. Mary's finding her stay here difficult enough as it is.'

'I know,' I interrupted, seizing my chance. 'You don't know how difficult! She doesn't think she can be helped. She thinks it's totally hopeless.' And I retold the story until I saw determination dawn on Sister's face. 'Leave it to me!' she promised, waving the cutting. 'I'll see what can be done.'

On the day of the remembered visit, Mrs McKenzie had arrived mid-morning and the screens were drawn round the bed rather ominously. We all got busy with newspapers or crosswords so that the screened figures might think we were gainfully employed and not eavesdropping on their conversation, but we were all aware of a low, rapid murmur, like cooing doves, punctuated by sudden gasps, fraught silences and a single sob. No familiar word struck the ear and I turned back to my newspaper, realising they were speaking in Gaelic.

At last Mrs McKenzie walked through the screens, wiping her eyes, and made for the duty room. The screens were removed and a tired Mary appeared. Her eyes were heavy and shadowed, but peaceful. She looked as if she had crossed a fatal bridge and laid down a great burden.

I was glad that she and her mother were reconciled, but disappointed that she still had little to hope for. Sister Lowther had been as good as her word and asked for Mary to be put into the INAH trial, but was told that she must finish her present course of streptomycin first. It was easy, apparently, for the TB bacillus to become resistant to the treatments if this was not done.

The newspaper report sent by Jean also went some way to explaining the strange behaviour of Oonagh McLeod, the teacher who insisted on lessons in the open air. Before World War II lessons *had* been provided for consumptive children in the Royal Victoria and these had taken place, as much as possible, in the open air. Perhaps Miss McLeod had simply seen her Hebridean island as one gigantic sanatorium and had stretched that 'as much as possible' into a completely Spartan existence in the snow-laden open air. If she had lost her own family from TB or even just witnessed the decimation around her at a time when cold and rest were the only treatments, her behaviour could and should be considered more heroic than eccentric or cruel. Hers were extreme tactics, but in a struggle against the wholesale extinction of her charges, she fought desperately and well.

At about this time changes at home were taking place. My young sister was about to leave school and start teacher-training and her prize-giving ceremony had contained a surprise: an announcement of the newly endowed *Etta More Memorial Prize for Drama,* won by a girl in Lou's class. The news reached me, and for silly reasons, as something of a shock. I felt severely shaken. The prize had been founded by my two best school friends.

Etta More was a girl in my year at Boroughmuir High School, although not in my class. She had died of consumption at the age of seventeen. When we first heard of her illness, these

94

particular two friends and I decided to form a visiting rota and one or other of us visited Etta several times a week in her pleasant little bedroom in a pretty village outside the city. Through circumstances outside their control the visits of the other two lessened and fell off, but I kept on visiting and last saw Etta two days before she died.

The prognosis had been that she would not last beyond six weeks from diagnosis. She had miliary TB, a very fast-acting form of the disease, but she actually lived on for six months. Would she have survived if she had been given the up-to-date chemotherapy which was then in its initial experimental stage? We all wondered.

On hearing the news of the prize, I found a mixture of conflicting feelings chasing through me with lightning speed. I felt a little bereft. Etta was my friend as well. I felt ousted from the cosy school triumvirate, which had so far seemed intact, as well as from the stump of the Etta More support group. It was the first time I had been left out of the loop. What had they been thinking about?

The answers came too in a steady stream. Why would they consult me when I had the same mortal disease? It would have been bizarre to ask me to contribute, which in any case I could not have done. Maybe it was even a placatory gesture to fate. 'You've taken Etta, you don't need another victim.' I tried to let it go, but it made me feel more isolated than before. Etta had been given a place in school history: mine was still pending.

And the first recipient of the *Etta More Memorial Prize*? It was Annette Crosbie, currently to be seen on television in a repeat of the comedy series, *One Foot in the Grave.* Annette was in my sister's class at Boroughmuir High School.

I turned to the safety valve of the hospital library book that I was reading, a light novel in the *David and Claudia* series, but even that comfort was denied me. The crew-cut doctor of the brisk instructions and warm, brown eyes arrived at my bedside with another doctor and picked it up.

'What's this?' he asked. 'Doesn't look much like Honours English to me. You should get hold of your reading-list and make better use of your time than this.'

How did he know I was doing Honours English and why should he give himself such paternalistic airs? I asked myself. He couldn't be more than five or six years older than I was – well, all right then, maybe nine or ten. The summer was already far advanced, I thought, looking out on the trees with leaves already turning from green to yellow; maybe he didn't realize that the reading list would have changed by the time it had any relevance to me. If I had been meant to return to study that year, they would have had to start raising my grades months before. The standard procedure was to spend a month at least on each grade and there were five of them.

What I did not realize at this time was that the Royal Victoria had unique links with Edinburgh University of many years' standing. The young Victorian Edinburgh doctor, Robert Philip, who had got to grips with the TB organism as soon as Koch discovered it in 1882, had gone on to found the unique system of treatment that ultimately made it possible to control the spread of the disease.

Part of his strategy had been to build a sanatorium within the bounds of Edinburgh and I was in it. From the time he became the first Professor of Tuberculosis, sanatorium and university were in constant dialogue. I was under the care of Sir Robert Philip's successor, Professor Cameron. Somebody *had* taken the trouble to find out what I was studying.

When the crew-cut doctor left, I didn't know what to do with myself; I felt rootless and aimless, afloat in a void yet buffeted. Better get the reading list, I supposed.

He was right, of course. The following week saw me deep into Shakeseare's *Othello* and strongly gratified by my retentive memory. *Othello* had been one of the final Shakespeare texts studied at school. My mind was several steps ahead of the printed page as the dialogue progressed. I shrank at the evil of Iago's revenge on Othello, mourned Othello's readiness to believe lies against his wife, admired Emilia's loyalty to Desdemona and shared Desdemona's bewilderment at Othello's violence.

As far as *David and Claudia* went, it was the difference between Noddy and King Lear. I felt like a greyhound in the slips with the barrier still to be lifted.

CHAPTER 9
Leaving My Little Wooden Hut

This feeling of extreme restlessness increased over the succeeding few weeks. I was now in a ward where half the patients were up for a large part of every day and the empty beds made the rest of us impatient for a similar change. The up patients would bring us news of the walks they had taken that morning, who had been at their dinner table, the places they had visited including the chalets and, crucially, what entertainment had just taken place or was coming their way on the following Wednesday evening. It made what was outside the ward more real. I felt I knew some of the people they talked about and looked forward to meeting them when and if it became possible.

There was a growing question mark in my mind, however. After fifteen months on bed rest with no overt symptoms of the disease except the pictures on x-rays – no cough, no sputum, and as far as I knew no positive results from either Blood Sediment Rate tests or gastric tests – I had begun to feel unwell. Not just the fatigue and melancholy that had been with me off and on for a number of months before diagnosis, the feeling that everything was futile. This was something different.

Witnessing the progress around me I had tried a little self-help therapy and put myself on Nurse Lucie's tonic – raw eggs in orange juice. To me it was revolting and, when I'd been taking it for a few days, I started to feel nauseated. Perhaps the raw eggs, coupled with a succession of hot, sunny days and a vivid imagination, were to blame for these symptoms. I began to fancy I was running a temperature and lay awake sometimes at night in a troubled frame of mind.

This intensified one day when I was told I was to see the professor. After such a long time on the back burner this was quite a shock. Professor Cameron, as I later found out, was supervising three sanitoria in Edinburgh, as well as a chest clinic, the TB dispensary, and a farm for training and occupational therapy.

All I knew at the time was that his visits to the Victoria were very rare. I had heard no stories of his sending for an individual patient. This was undoubtedly the crunch. He was going to tell me that I had relapsed and must begin again at the beginning.

With only a small locker each to stow our worldly goods, I had no clothes to change into so the only concession I could make to this important interview was to belt my pink woollen dressing-gown round me. I was placed in a wheelchair – which, of course, added to my fears – and pushed into the main building, where I came face to face with the great man. Or rather, face to knee since I was still seated and he was quite tall.

He was pleasant and unhurried, but his manner was weighty. Something was afoot.

To my surprise, his questions, once we were seated on the same level, were not about my health, but my university career. I was assuming that this chat was a social preliminary to the real subject, when he startled me into sitting bolt upright.

'How would you feel about starting again in the new term?' he asked.

That was a mere month away. As the question sank in, I could not see how it would be possible. I answered that it would be marvellous, though with some trepidation remembering the 'home in time for Christmas' anecdote. In view of my recent fears of a pulmonary breakdown, the promise of movement seemed doubly incredible. I would have liked to ask why everyone else had to prepare for a return to activity over five months when I was being asked to do it in one, but the professor answered my unasked question, surprising me by the trouble he had taken to enquire into my situation.

'Your lectures,' he said, 'will all be in the morning.' (Even I did not know this.) 'This will mean that you will go to bed for two hours every afternoon and this is something you must keep up until further notice.'

I made no protest. Half liberation was much much better than no liberation. Besides I was already, when vertical, suffering from a dragging pain in my back, just under my right shoulder-blade. It was probably caused by the weight of my still-collapsed lung. I would be glad of a rest in the afternoon. Reluctantly I gave up my vision of noisy afternoon meetings with friends and the quiet and mental rigour of library study.

The professor's further instructions were that I should get up straight away for Entertainments (Grade 2), for lunch every day the following week (Grade 3), and be up fully apart from rest hour in the week following that, (Grade 4). An hour's rest in the afternoon was obligatory for all patients.

I was wheeled back to the ward in a daze, unable to take in this complete change in fortune. My wardmates were equally stunned. Never had they heard of such lightning promotion. They looked at me with something like awe. It seems to me now, with hindsight, that the new treatment was already being acknowledged as a cure by the doctors spear-heading its application, or perhaps I was part of the experiment to prove that it was so.

I tried a few practice runs at getting out of bed when the nurses' backs were turned but was always glad to lie down afterwards to ease the niggle in my back.

To be up for Entertainments was a big deal with an odd name. On Wednesday evenings of each week something of a hopefully entertaining nature was provided. Whist drives and concerts were the staples.

'What else besides Wednesdays?' I asked.

'You can attend the morning service on Sundays,' came the answer. Well, most of my friends were toying with atheism and I was, at that time, a born-again agnostic. We knew, or thought we knew, that Darwin was right and the Bible was far from the whole story. There were those who alleged that indeed it was *all* story and nothing else. But it was going a bit far, even for me, to file the Almighty under 'Entertainment'. I made up my mind to present myself on Sunday morning in a receptive frame of mind, but first there was Wednesday.

We all turned up at the appointed time in the large social room with a stage – or at least a dais – at one end. John Levey had volunteered to meet me and had kept me a place. There was not an unsmiling face anywhere and I was introduced to a few people, all male, who had previously been outside my orbit. One was a genial middle-aged, balding man with glasses and twinkling eyes and there was a younger one about my own age who was in the hospital, not with TB, but with an entirely different long-term chest complaint. He was waiting for surgery.

Two of these three were born comedians and the laughter was copious and easy. I was enjoying this and was curious to see the star of the show, Jimmy Shand, who had become a BBC legend. This was unusual for one so easily linked to the unsophisticated tartan and heather label, but if ever I saw a man who transcended his own trappings, Jimmy Shand was that man.

He was not visually imposing. He was born poor, spent some years in the mines, and suffered from ill health most of his life. He was very thin and very shy, but from the moment his fingers touched the accordion he was totally in command of the stage and his audience. His eyes were bent with grim determination on the ground. To look up would have been to risk meeting another pair of eyes. There was no introduction. He just played.

Where had he gone, I wondered, seeing his bent head and flying fingers, but soon had the answer. My usually undemonstrative toes were keeping time to the music like everybody else's. He was communicating, sending out messages through the music. He *was* the music. He was the jig, the strathspey, the reel; *The Gay Gordons, The Flowers of Edinburgh* and *Drops o' Brandy.*

It was a very long time since anyone in this audience had danced but with the inescapable joy and precision of the beat, we were all dancing again or at least our fingers, toes and hearts were. By the time we had mentally danced them all, we were tired but exhilarated, without having lifted a foot from the floor.

Shand maintained a very modest account of himself in interviews and in print, stating, 'I was never meant to be an entertainer.' But a man who drew a crowd of 20,000 in a single appearance and stopped traffic in the process, and whose music brought one of his young fans out of a coma after a serious accident, is something more than an entertainer. He has entered the realm of legend. Shand was known for complete dedication to his music, total self-effacement and a determined absence of spin. When asked to describe a recent trip, 550 miles south to Southsea, he merely said, 'We arrived at Southsea, did the dancin', cam back up tae Muchty.'

His portrait hangs in The National Portrait Gallery. His statue stands in his much-loved home-town, Auchtermuchty, in the Kingdom of Fife.

On the Sunday morning we assembled again, but not all of us. Not everyone was of the same religious denomination. John Levey, for instance, was Jewish. Still it was quite a substantial gathering. I prepared myself to be spiritually fed.

It was a dull overcast morning, but the sermon shook me out of my lethargy. It was a blistering attack on worldly excesses – or pleasures as the padre called them – and those who indulged in them. Just that week some of us had been exchanging notes on the length of our stay in our single-sex, single-bedded, always-supervised wards as well as the austerity of the food and no-nonsense surroundings. Some patients had enjoyed these pleasures for years. We dared not look up at the padre in case we exploded with rage or derision or incredulous amusement.

Once in the open we enjoyed repeating some of the more sonorous phrases and wondered why this spare, sad figure of a padre had felt that such a sermon was relevant in a sanatorium. We came to the conclusion he was trying out a sermon intended for some other congregation. We were either guinea-pigs or write-offs to him.

In the main we were blessed in our various men of the cloth. My Mr D was a regular visitor, offering constant interest and support. One day we had got on to the topic of the impressive, almost incredible, rate of change in the nineteenth and twentieth centuries. We had measured it by the amount of railway track laid during the lifetime of Robert Browning; 12 miles when he was born to 140,000 when he died. We had measured it by the move from the first horseless carriage to the dawn of the space age. Finally I said, to clinch the matter, 'I'm always surprised that...' I had been going to say, 'there are people still alive who remember Queen Victoria,' but did a lightning sum in my head, realized Mr D was one of them and managed a rapid change of topic. We chatted on for a couple of minutes and I thought I had skirted the rapids nicely, but after he had said his goodbyes, he put his head round the door again. 'And, of course, dear, I remember Queen Victoria.' He chuckled and left.

Looking back at my twenty-year-old self I am startled at my own, youthful arrogance. More than half a century later, there are still people alive, one or two, who might remember Queen Victoria. I remember her quite well myself from a tattered memoir, passed to me by a former neighbour, which recorded her total disbelief that the Duke of Wellington was dead. She knew it couldn't be so because he would have let her know.

The other clergyman who visited the ward regularly was the Roman Catholic priest, a refreshing character. He freely discussed wine, horse-racing and betting with his parishioners and always made sure that he visited all the beds in the small ward, making us feel important.

On the following Wednesday the entertainment was a whist drive and I won a bottle of perfume. It was a flattish, disc-shaped bottle of 4711 Eau-de-Cologne considered very stylish at the time. The Americans during the war had accustomed us to the glamour of numbers, with Glen Miller's *Pennsylvania 6-5000* and other pieces. So it was quite contemporary on the one hand. On the other it took me right back to pre-war Christmases and the sudden appearance of a flattish, disc-shaped whisky bottle with its golden cargo – a symbol of good cheer to usher in the New Year. Things were looking up. In fact the pace of life was going into overdrive.

On the same evening I had the pleasure of introducing Isla, now promoted to Grade 2, to John. She looked very striking in a light summer dress and an eye-catching gold bracelet that nearly ended their friendship before it had begun. Analysing the evening afterwards she referred to John's big-headedness and arrogance.

'What makes you say that?' I asked

'Well,' she said, 'he asked me, "What's this you've been trying to show me all night?" and made to grab my wrist. I wasn't showing him at all. My arm was behind my back.'

Maybe it was different in a family without brothers, I thought, recognising a male gambit. Wanting these two friends to like each other, I embarked on an oil-pouring operation. 'Yes, you should have seen your face!' I said. 'He was joking; he was only saying it to wind you up.'

Privately I thought he was only saying it because he wanted to know her better. He was attracted to her flamboyant good looks. I succeeded in interpreting them so well to each other that they were soon quite close, so close in fact that I feared I might be losing two friends.

I, on the other hand, was quickly receding from Isla's immediate neighbourhood; I had been moved out to one of the two-bedded chalets along with a girl called Amy from another ward. This was another move towards independence and I was glad to be able to enjoy my brief time there in the late summer weather.

When the nurse carrying my few belongings had pointed me to my allotted bed and gone, I took stock. Not at first of my surroundings, although I felt I was expanding in this bare unadorned space. Amy had not yet arrived and I was enjoying being alone for the first time in months. No matter how supportive my wardmates had been, no matter how enjoyable their company, there had been a need for continuous response to conversation, questions, needs, and comment of every kind. It was not often possible to plumb your own thoughts in a few minutes' silence without attracting notice from someone. Now my needy inner self could stretch and breathe in peace.

In time I took in three walls of tongued and grooved wood of a lively brown, with a window set in each. Two beds were placed against the side walls flanked by the usual lockers at the head. There was just room for a single small chair at the foot of each bed. The side windows were fully open on what was a balmy September day to various aspects of the wards and walkways of the hospital, but the view in front of the chalet through the missing wall was glorious and interrupted by nothing except wheeling birds. Acres of green lawn lined with trees stretched to what seemed like the horizon, although I knew that the suburb of a busy city lay in the dip beyond the furthest trees. I felt I was breathing powerfully and deeply.

To my amazement the chalets were not really cold at all, not in comparison with the high-ceilinged, wind-tunnel wards. At that time of year, they were downright cosy and, even if we had to sleep with tarpaulins on our beds to avoid being soaked with dew, there were compensations. We could watch the dawn and sunset in perfect peace and study the birds at closer quarters.

We noticed that they disappeared ten minutes before the visitors were due to appear and arrived back ten minutes before it was time for them to go. It looked as if they might have a spy network covering the Edinburgh bus system and its travellers.

In the short time that I was there I came to love the privacy that my chalet offered. The hospital was behind us, visible through the little rear window but, thanks to our better state of health, we went there for meals and treatment rather than being visited by the nurses and doctors. No one bothered us and I saw that the longer-term patients had developed close, supportive and friendly relationships with their neighbours. There was a lot of warmth and laughter. I was, of course, in a hurry to pick up the reins at home and college again, but part of me wanted to linger there enjoying the novelty of the experience.

Amy was a large-framed girl with slightly drawn features and an interesting problem. Her mother was a very large lady – twenty-three stone at a time when obesity was rare. When, on visiting days, she took the single step up into the chalet, it sagged at the side she was on and I could feel my position in bed altering from flat on my back to reclining on my side like a Roman Senator at a banquet.

Amy was sensibly aware that her mother overdid things a bit, but she was facing a possible life-or-death decision as a result. Her father, knowing we were all supposed to be stoking up on food to give our bodies a better chance, had advised Amy to look the other way when the plates came round in case she ended up weighing twenty-three stone. Amy looked at me, an elder sister figure, and I looked helplessly back.

'At least wait till you're well and home again. You might never get fat anyway,' I suggested, knowing that as soon as the weather cooled again, the question would resolve itself. We were usually so cold that our appetites were fairly ravenous, with a hunger that our still scanty rations could not satisfy.

I was astonished at the phenomenon of my own newly discovered appetite! Food had been a lifetime problem for me. From daily child-mother tussles to wasted school-dinner money, I did not want food. I was sixteen before I felt a single pang of hunger and now, suddenly, I was wishing for tea-time with its weak tea and thin bread and butter. Come to think of it, the liquid in the cup was not always the pale, greyish, milky colour of weak tea. At regular intervals, probably monthly, it became a vague purple and tasted strangely metallic. I once asked Peggy Robson about it and she said it happened on the days the urns were cleaned.

My newly awakened appetite should have meant an increase in weight but in fact I never gained an ounce. However much I ate, my weight remained stubbornly the same. The years I spent trying to increase my constant 7 stone 2 pounds and failing to do it have given me a strong respect for the wisdom of the human body. I was on the point of motherhood, years later, before I achieved a significant weight gain.

Lying awake after a spectacular sunset the night before I was to go home, I thought about the little universe of the hospital, where I was now on the edge, ready to spring into the bigger one outside the Victoria's walls. The scene before me, while I could still see it, was a tranquil one of well-maintained lawns bordered by trees. Thanks to the gentle slope that the sanatorium was built on I was aware of the boundlessness beyond. What it held would be revealed to me in time, but I knew that there would be some turbulence not too far away. This peaceful enclave had sheltered me during one disrupted, difficult year of my life. I had been guided and guarded and mended here, although no one acted as though this was more than a running repair. The amazing knowledge that our lethal disease could be cured was a cause for rejoicing that was still in the future.

Now I was going out again into the Great Unknown, but with the gentle family interface to ease the transition. My long-suffering sister, Louise, turned up at the appointed time with a taxi. I had said goodbye to Amy and the birds and had done the rounds of my recently occupied ward, but Isla was nowhere to be seen. This didn't really matter, I thought; I would be coming back on weekly visits for my air refills and would bump into her then.

In actual fact I never saw her again. When I heard on the grapevine that she and John were to be married, I thought them very brave. No-one at that time would have given much for their chance of a long life together but, as things have turned out, there is every chance that they have enjoyed just that. I hope that it is so

Once in the taxi, it struck me that I did not know the way home. I had come here on my first visit to the Royal Victoria Hospital for Tuberculosis in an ambulance with tinted windows. I could see out but nobody could see in. I was glad of this. I had felt very self-conscious sitting on a leather bench by myself. The driver was in his own separate cab. It was a peculiarly embarrassing situation and my mind had turned inwards, failing to register the unfamiliar roads that the ambulance was taking. I had felt a little fraudulent, to tell the truth; ambulances were for dramatic emergencies and very sick people. It was only a little shadow, for goodness' sake!

I looked round as the taxi sped down the drive. Leaving seemed inconclusive, odd, unsettling, low-key. The mood of the staff had been one of only cautious optimism. I turned once to look back at the entrance we had just passed through and started to memorise the way home.

CHAPTER 10
Bearding the Black Douglas

There was very little time left before the onslaught of the new term. I sorted out my clothes, found a high-necked sleeveless jumper and a Gor-Ray skirt and braved a bus-trip into town. I had invented a reason for going, but the real one was to stretch my wings and make sure there was air under them.

The journey was full of memories. We passed Balgreen Library that I had visited every week as a child, Saughton Park with its wide avenue of beeches, chaotic Gorgie Road where a dentist had cracked a perfectly good tooth of mine and Ardmillan Cemetery with its high stone walls where a neighbour had dreamed she was laying linoleum.

We passed the *West End* where the road broadened into Princes Street. I would get off at The Mound, halfway along, by the Scottish National Gallery. Maybe I would be able to jump off the bus before it came to a halt. I used to have the knack in that previous life that I was now returning to.

It was while making the jump that my whole world changed. I caught sight of my bare, slug-white legs in mid-leap. They were in complete contrast to the shining golden ones that the journey had thrust on my attention. In a street like Princes Street, more French boulevard than highway, golden legs stretched in a long unbroken line of assurance from the West End to Waverley Station. I would have fallen, if I had not been falling already. I had leapt from one world and landed in another.

Nylons had been in short supply when I fell ill and it was still considered perfectly respectable, an accepted fact of post-war austerity, to have bare legs. During my absence nylons had taken great strides, so to speak. Bare legs would no longer do. I had some catching up to do.

How much had changed I did not realize until I entered the lecture-hall in the following week. A larger than usual gathering of students, all anxious to be counted present on the first day of the university term, looked eagerly around. Some of them would be hoping that early attendance would earn Brownie points for the whole year.

They were all very young. I had to remind myself that I was only a year older than they were. But that was not the whole of the difference. The walls were still chocolate brown and battleship grey and looked likely to remain so, a possibly proud plank in the platform of tradition. The difference was that in this class, in this whole intake, there were no ex-servicemen to be seen, no duffle coats, no neutral or disillusioned expressions. I felt like Rip Van Winkle. Or some kind of ghost maybe. A revenant. Would anyone on the campus recognize me?

A short time later we, the newly decanted class, were pouring down one wide set of steps in the main building when, against the odds, it happened; my name was called. Across the well of the stairs on the upward flight was my big-hearted friend, Grace.

'Come for a coffee!' she yelled.

'Can't,' I yelled back, 'I have a class.'

'Cut it!'

'Can't.' I knew that if I didn't break this new and very hard ground on the first day, I never would. There were things I had promised myself to do.

'I need to ask you something,' she shouted. 'Meet me at three on the library steps!' and she was gone.

Grace had supported me at almost every turn during my illness and had made many a visit, with and without Neill, her student boyfriend, both to my home and the sanatorium. How could I refuse? Besides she had gone mysteriously off my radar for the past three months and I wanted to find out what she'd been doing.

So much for rest hour, I thought, as I reached my next class and found a seat.

The crunch was coming. It was time for the big decision. The first two years doing Honours English were wide-based, with equally balanced courses in English language and English literature. Those I had already done. In the third year we had to commit ourselves to one or the other for the following two years. For an hour I put on a show of listening, but my mind was miles away.

The class just attended in English language had been a ground-clearing operation towards a decision, but I was not rushing at anything. I stayed behind after the preliminary introduction to the coming course for a word with the Language Professor, Angus McIntosh, a charismatic Scot with an Oxford accent. He seemed pleased to pick up matters where they had rested sixteen months earlier and said he hoped that I would be going on with my studies in the Language Department. I answered that it was good to know I would be welcome, but I must first speak to my former literature tutor. He gave me a quizzical look, but gallantly squired me across the quadrangle to the room of the Black Douglas.

I felt bad dissembling as I was already quite clear in my own mind that I was going to read literature. If my life was not going to be a long one, as the pattern of TB suggested, I was going to spend it doing what I wanted to do, as far as possible, instead of what might seem logical. A track record of merits and distinctions such as I had in English language would make sure of a really good degree, but I was less interested in the mechanics of English than the exciting content of literature. Nevertheless, something did hang in the balance, and it had to be resolved in order to clear the ground.

'Here's Miss Strahan back to see you,' Professor McIntosh began. 'I think she should have spent the past year in Switzerland, but she's not been so far away from us after all, and here she is and we're all glad to see her back.' I had a fleeting pang at the thought that I would be moving out of the orbit of this warm and civilised man. When he had gone, the Black Douglas looked at me with the same polite half-smile he had worn when Professor McIntosh was speaking. We had moved into the larger teaching room where I had so often sat in acute distress a lifetime ago. Without the burly figures and silent presence of my former fellow-tutees, it looked somehow lighter. The Black Douglas had even shrunk a little. In a few seconds his smile had turned to a look of mild enquiry.

'I'm thinking,' I said, 'of withdrawing from the Honours English Class. I don't seem to be quite up to it.' I got no further.

'Oh no!' he said. 'You mustn't do that! I never meant you to think that. There's plenty of talent there. *Plenty.* You'll walk it. You really must not *do* that!'

I was surprised at the intensity of his reaction even while being cheered by his frank admission that I was neither lazy nor stupid. There was definitely something out of kilter here.

'But,' I protested, 'you've always given me such low marks.' *And,* I might have added, diminished me, misrepresented and insulted me on every possible occasion. I managed, however, to swallow the fighting words.

'I know,' he nodded, as if inviting me to collude in a reasonable course of action.

I waited for his further explanation – and kept on waiting. Normally I would have rushed to fill the uncomfortable gap, as I had done in his tutorials in the past, but this time I felt the discomfort was his and well-deserved and said nothing.

Finally he said, 'Yes, I thought you were cocky and just needed taking down a peg or two.'

I could not believe my ears. He was admitting to having betrayed his position and my trust, to tampering with my marks for some sick reason of his own and, although I knew that he had done this, I had not expected to hear such a frank confession of delinquency.

Cockiness, whatever it was, was not something that I had ever before been accused of. A shy manner and a too soft voice were. What had I ever done to make him think I was 'cocky'? The most forward thing I had done was to try to answer the questions he had set his students. Perhaps in his eyes I was not a student. Perhaps he felt that a university education was for men only. He was perfectly congenial to the male students in the group.

'You certainly must not think of giving up!' he said with a final curt nod.

I turned and left, saying nothing. There was no point; we did not speak the same language. To conclude that he had apologised to me would, I think, have been wide of the mark. His nod could as easily have meant, 'See how powerful I am! See what I did to you!'

Nevertheless I felt freed of a burden as I walked down the shallow steps of *the Old Quad* to my first English literature lecture of the year. I had asked for an explanation and had got one – of sorts. I had made a bully own up and, now that he had done that, my decision to read literature seemed both desirable and logical. I was vindicated.

My illness had given me a truer perspective on things and also the courage to be assertive when I needed to be.

I was eager to get home and rest my back, but first came the meeting with Grace. I spent the intervening hours in the library looking for a couple of textbooks and was lucky enough to find one and make some notes. Essential texts were often in very short supply, but we all tried to borrow rather than buy.

It was good to see Grace outside the hospital ambience again. Her smile was as bright as ever. She explained that her parents' death a few years before and her elder brother's busy life in a new post meant that she was left with the job of bringing up her young brother, Harry, a responsibility that she took seriously but wore lightly.

'Only it's made me a bit busy for seeing you,' she apologised.

'Oh Grace, don't be silly!' I rushed in, 'You've given me so much already. It's time the boot was on the other foot.'

'Well,' she said, 'I was coming to that. Can you be ready for a long day trip in July?'

'Probably,' I agreed. 'What for?'

'Well, you know, Neill doesn't want to wait any longer, now that he's landed this post in Glasgow.'

'Oh Grace, that's great!' I said. I had watched the progress of their romance from light flirtation to close commitment. Neill, a broad-shouldered figure with reddish hair and a formidable mind for debate, had never dropped the flirtatious manner in whatever direction he chose to deploy it. This very public gesture was no light decision. And he would never be richer than on his wedding day. They were a well-matched pair. They were moving to Glasgow within a few months and were planning their wedding for the following July.

'And could you,' she went on, 'do the same trip next Wednesday morning?'

Seeing my hesitation, she looked anxious. 'I wouldn't normally ask when you're still settling in, but I'm selling up here and there's a legal appointment that afternoon that I just have to keep. The solicitor can't give me any other day. I need somebody to take Harry to Kelvinside Academy for an admissions exam. Could you do it?'

'Of course,' I rashly agreed, glad of the chance to repay some of the support I had enjoyed for the past year. There was a difficulty in that I knew nobody in my new classes well enough to ask for a set of notes. I repeated to myself the mantra of a religious friend. The Lord would provide.

I had never been in Glasgow on my own, never mind with a young protégé, but managed by train and taxi to deliver my charge in good time. In the two hours that he was occupied I found a bus route to the centre of the city and knocked on my grandmother's door.

She had had thirteen children, as many people did in her young day without the benefit of family planning clinics or easily available contraceptive devices. With so many children, she could have been excused for looking vague when grandchildren turned up at her door, but she was delighted to see me.

According to family lore she said, 'Oh, my God!' and I said, 'No, your grand-daughter.'

Soon we were happily exchanging hospital stories and showing off our scars. She had recently undergone heroic surgery to remove her gall bladder and I had to admit that my two finger-tip sized circles were no competition at all.

By the end of the day trip I was well into my urban stride.

The year of stasis was over.

CHAPTER 11
An End to an Old Song?

1950-1951 was the year in which my story coincided with the story of the fight against TB. Not that it ended there, but inevitably my distance from the cutting edge of that experience increased. I kept on with my appointments for weekly refills of air at the Royal Victoria for a year to eighteen months longer, but life was so busy that my visits to the wards and chalets quickly became fewer.

My final visit to the Royal Victoria Hospital for Tuberculosis was quite unexpected. I was in a state of relapse at the time and being treated with PAS and isoniazid when I was told, with typical brevity, that I need no longer attend for refills of air. Looking on the bright side, I might have assumed that my lung had repaired itself, but this was given the lie by the sachets and tablets in my handbag. I think it had become clear to those treating the condition that chemotherapy was so much more effective than other treatments that it could be relied on to improve matters without more invasive methods.

The relapses are also something I understand better with newly acquired knowledge. It had become obvious, through the work of Professor John Crofton's team operating from

Edinburgh during the 1950s, that the TB bacillus was killed off faster with more than a single form of chemotherapy. I had been treated first with streptomycin and para-amino salicylic acid which gave it a good knock on the head, but not a permanent one. Later treatment was with para-amino salicylic acid and isoniazid with the same result. It needed more than that.

Dr. John Crofton, appointed Professor of Tuberculosis at Edinburgh University in 1952 and later knighted for his services to medicine, settled on a therapeutic treatment that combined a *trio* of drugs, a practice still in use today. Sometimes a fourth item from the pharmacopeia has to be added to the cocktail.

Sir John Crofton, as he became, headed up the team whose close monitoring of every situation in the treatment of tuberculosis has led to the spectacular control of this formerly lethal disease in this country and provided the knowledge for control on a world scale. Using the Edinburgh System first devised by Sir Robert Philip in the 1880s and 90s, he applied his knowledge of new, potent antibiotics to the greatest advantage.

To quote a recent authority on the subject of achieving this control:

> *...there were also two great leaps. The first was the organization of a planned and co-ordinated tuberculosis service. The second was the organization and practice of rational chemo-therapy. The latter could not have succeeded so dramatically as it did without the former. It is through such propitious chronological relationships that advancing history is made.*
>
> *One Hundred Years of the Co-ordinated Service for Tuberculosis,* Christopher Clayson (Edinburgh 1988)

As it turned out for me, one last despairing writhe of the monster gave way to half a century of largely untroubled health.

I have come to see 1950-1951 as the precise turning point in the treatment of TB in the United Kingdom. It was the year of belt, braces and two pairs of pants. A couple of years earlier I might have missed treatment with effective drugs. A year later I would have missed the great freeze; the bloodless fingers and toes and aching muscles, the open, foggy windows and empty grate. Several years later I would have missed all surgical procedures which were by then regarded as an unnecessary evil. However, who is to say that we were any the worse for being subjected to all three treatments?

It was, of course, an experience that has stayed with me up to the present day. And of course it has surfaced from time to time. One such occasion was when I rang my G.P. in the 1970s for the results of a largely routine x-ray. There was a minute's delay while he fetched the letter, then a lengthy crinkling sound as he withdrew it from the envelope and unfolded it.

'Ye-es,' he said in a tone of some gravity. 'Same old story.' There followed a long pause while I noticed that my hands were sweating, something that hadn't happened since adolescence. 'Healed deposits. You can forget it.' He was referring to the knots of white scarring showing where a lesion had been.

Forget it, however, is not a wholly likely scenario and I have found my knowledge and understanding of the bug growing over the years, fuelled by random books, as well as those recommended by helpful medical friends and, of course, the internet. I have discovered that I was hugely favoured as well as hugely lucky. As a result I have enjoyed the proverbial wealth beyond the dreams of avarice.

It would be foolish to deny that there are some disadvantages to living with the enemy, including the very real existence of stigma. I was well protected by my sensitive family from this and it was some time before I realised how extensive and destructive this process was. It was shocking, in particular, to read of the attitudes to tuberculosis and the poor, i.e. those without independent means, that were current at the start of the twentieth century.

Sir James Kingston Fowler, writing in 1923, states much of the policy that prevailed and was sadly influential at the time. Occupation for the sufferer from consumption was held to be advisable and he saw walking as a suitable occupation for people of private means, but added:

> *People in sanatoria from the 'industrial class' cannot be given unlimited freedom of movement for reasons upon which it is unnecessary to dwell.*

Marcus Paterson, Medical Superintendent at Frimley Sanatorium in its early days, had started a regime of hard manual labour for patients there as early as 1905, the so-called 'pickaxe cure for TB'. His patients, men and women, graduated from ten-mile walks to digging with light spades and moving on to heavier ones. They dug by hand a reservoir for 500,000 gallons of water, laid concrete paths, cleared fire-breaks, felled trees and built a concrete walk-way from one department to another. He claimed they benefited greatly from their labours:

> *Then the sanatorium, which was too often the home of neurotic individuals, mentally and physically deteriorated by periods of ease and idleness, was transformed into a workshop of busy, hopeful men and women.*

An American doctor in 1910 hoped to expand the regime to

> *certain classes of criminals, dipsomaniacs, drug fiends... those exhibiting degenerative symptoms.*

119

Many natural human activities were forbidden to the poorer patients, whose only offence had been to contract an infectious disease. Amongst them were: visiting and receiving visits, conversation, laughter, singing and whistling. Eating between meals was allowed, but only with written permission. They were not allowed to go on the designated walks enjoyed by patients of independent means. These were clearly marked in green and red to prevent any chance meeting of the sexes by those who were allowed to use them.

Naturally many patients preferred to take their chances outside the sanatoria, but soldiers returning from war and hospitalized for TB expected better treatment after the service they had given to their country and were more voluble in their protests. At first they were threatened with curtailment of their pensions unless they conformed to sanatorium regulations, but common sense finally won the day.

Better attitudes have, of course, prevailed and today we live in a more equal society. The most overt example of repressive treatment that I witnessed took place after my spell as an in-patient in the Victoria and was in no way comparable, although it is perhaps possible to discern survivals of these earlier savage impositions and embargoes in attitudes still surviving into the 1950s.

In the Royal Victoria in the early 1950s, after an illicit get-together, a directive had gone out that male and female patients were not to speak to one another. One female patient, enjoying a game of putting on the lawn, dared to answer a question called from a window on a male ward. The offence was relayed from the nurse on duty on the questioner's ward to the sister on duty on the female ward of the offender and retribution was swift. The offender's putting-stick was confiscated, causing much hilarity for days afterwards.

Naturally fear had become the ruling reaction to any mention of TB in the first half of the twentieth century and resulting prejudice was and is slow to shift. My reaction was to ignore it and strike a blow for common sense by mentioning TB on every occasion when it would be natural to do so.

It is worth repeating that many more people have been in contact with the TB bug than those who become ill with it. This can now be very accurately measured by the Mantoux test and I remember being told, when I was ill in 1950, that fewer than 10% of the population had escaped contact with the TB bacillus. Several decades later the figure of those who had not met the bug had risen to 30%, a happy result of the fall in infection. It might be possible, given a benevolent world dictator, to reduce the risk of infection to nil. Meantime what can be done in difficult circumstances is being done. But there is no denying that the spread of HIV throughout the world has complicated things in recent years by weakening the sufferers' immune systems and leaving them vulnerable to tuberculosis and, of course, other ailments including leprosy. The battle is not yet over.

On a recent trip back to Edinburgh, I found myself in a spot I recognized immediately. It was the outer wall of the Royal Victoria grounds. From my vantage point in the car I saw something I had not noticed before, a thin line of gravestones round the northern perimeter. They looked like a loosely thrown lasso separating the sanatorium from the world outside, a *cordon sanitaire* for the city, a protective haven for the benighted souls inside.

A series of pictures of my life passed rapidly before my eyes, the life that I might not have had, had things followed the old path: my lace wedding dress foaming on its hanger; my husband waiting at the altar – and all these years later speaking to our friends at our recent Golden Wedding anniversary; our miraculous daughters; our first grandchild and the five that followed; the thousands of students I was privileged to teach; the thousands of books that I have read; the few that I have written. All things that would not have happened before the development of successful chemotherapy.

Then different images took shape: the army of scientists, doctors and nurses involved in caring for the victims of this lethal condition in all the centuries leading up to its conquest. I mentally traced the steps (from cupping and bleeding to freezing the patient, the use of the knife and, finally, successful chemotherapy) that had made tuberculosis or phthisis or consumption less *the captain of all these men of death,* as John Bunyan put it, and more of a brief interruption in the lives of a few unfortunates.

Then one last time I looked at the gravestones stretching into the distance, looked up at the sunny blue sky with its little white clouds, and felt a savage joy that the march of the markers of death had at last been checked.

Not long ago – a matter of months – I heard that an old college friend of my elder brother, Ned, was suffering from cancer and not expected to live. He was aware of this and I felt that I had to write to him, saying at the end of my letter that time had seen off most of the wine glasses that he gave us as a wedding present, but that we still had two left and had toasted him in a glass of wine. He was pleased at this and countered that on one of his visits to us in Edinburgh decades ago he had thought, because of my fragile appearance, that I 'had not long to go' and had always been pleased to find out how wrong he was.

No, you do not discern an early love affair. If we were in love with anything, it was with life. I am only one of the millions who have been spared the tragedy of bowing out of life too early. This is thanks to the devoted efforts of the man who set up the machinery for diagnosis and control, to the men who discovered and shaped the antibiotic treatment now so successful, and to the very propitious stroke of fortune that brought their efforts together.

EPILOGUE

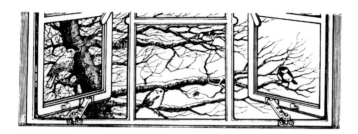

There has been such unease in recent years about the return of TB that it seems useful to put this broadly in perspective for the reader.

Firstly, a patient diagnosed today with Mycobacterium Tuberculosis (TB) or consumption or phthisis, as the disease is also known, would recover much more rapidly. The powerful antibiotics administered would render the bug powerless and the patient non-infectious, possibly in a fortnight, certainly within a month.

There would then be a more prolonged period of recovery, while the site of the lesion repaired itself, but during this period the patient would not normally need to be absent from work, school or the domestic front. Recovery (and the doctors no longer hesitate at the word 'cure') would be a case of 'medicine and duty.'

So why the panic and media warnings? Well, for one thing this resilient and nearly indestructible bacillus has a marvellous capacity to adapt and survive. It has been killing since the days of the dinosaurs and readily becomes resistant to the current chemotherapy. We are staying in the lead by finding new effective medicines while we can, but must ask ourselves if this can go on for ever. If not, what happens when the music stops?

The long-term aim of healers and scientists over the centuries has been to eradicate the scourge, as we have done, for example, with that other killer, smallpox. In Britain, it has to be said, we are nearly there. So nearly there, in fact, that all the sanatoria closed or went into use for other purposes in the 1960s. So close that the number of deaths from TB has remained at fewer than one per hundred thousand of the population (1:100,000) since 1985. This compares with 306:100,000 in the nineteenth century, when the Bronte sisters wrote triumphantly about love before TB cut short their lives. From 1850 to the year 1910, four million people in Britain died of tuberculosis; an average of 66,666 deaths per year.

Can it become fact, the total eradication of this age-old superbug? The answer at the moment would have to be No. We are indeed an island, but air, land and sea bridges have breached that isolation and most of us would not have it otherwise. This determined linkage to the rest of the world means that we have millions upon millions of people to exchange germs with. Eradication of the TB bug would be constantly overtaken by re-infection because treatment elsewhere on the globe is less thorough, less effective and less well funded than it is here.

For the excellent tradition in British TB treatment we have to thank a visionary Scottish doctor, an Edinburgh son of the manse, Robert W. Philip, later *Sir* Robert W. Philip, 1857-1939. As a newly qualified doctor, just graduated from Edinburgh University, he visited Vienna in 1882 and studied under Robert Koch, who had just succeeded in identifying the TB bacillus and demonstrating it under the microscope. For the first time, direct efforts to control and destroy the organism could be made. It was a giant step towards knowing the enemy.

Philip was excited and horrified in equal parts. This proof of an infective agent meant that the possibilities of the spread of the disease were boundless. Control could only be achieved in the individual cases that came to light, unless some other method of coping could be devised.

On his own initiative, without encouragement and sometimes in the face of opposition, he devised a system for identifying patients, examining and advising their families and other contacts, nursing and isolating active cases in sanatoria, ensuring rest, fresh air and a healthy diet.

The core of his Edinburgh System, as it came to be known, consisted of three main buildings: a clinic or dispensary in the heart of Edinburgh for advising families and dispensing medicine, an actual sanatorium, unusual in being within the Edinburgh City boundaries, and a farm, a short distance away, to provide therapeutic employment in the open air and to train for further employment in a life-sustaining environment. We are, of course, speaking of a time when most men earned their living manually and could not afford to abandon physical labour.

Philip laid his plan before the government of the day to a marked lack of interest and was forced to lobby 'a few kind friends' to provide the money to set it up. The dispensary was equipped in 1887, Queen Victoria's Jubilee year, by donors ready to mark the occasion by honouring the queen in this way. Both the dispensary and the sanatorium, opened in 1904, were given her name and known respectively as the Royal Victoria Dispensary for Tuberculosis and the Royal Victoria Hospital for Tuberculosis, the very hospital where I spent so many months in 1950-1951. The main building was a lovely, slightly Gothic, old Georgian building, Craigleith House.

Without realising it at the time, I was being treated at the fountainhead of wisdom in the fight against TB. Edinburgh University boasted the first Professor of Tuberculosis, Sir Robert Philip himself, and it was his successor who directed our treatment. Since the aim was to gather the facts in order to improve treatment and reduce mortality, we were very closely monitored and nursed.

It was part of Philip's plan to prove that it was possible to nurse the condition successfully within the confines of a city, in this way giving confidence to people seeking help and providing a less isolated existence for patients. It must have taken much of the fear out of what people still regarded as a life sentence.

It is difficult to comprehend the difference his decision made to patients and their relatives and friends. Any pre-existing TB hospitals had been sited deep in rural areas, which were difficult or impossible to reach as well as expensive. Here is a description of arrival at the sanatorium in Loggerheads by a new patient:

> *When we turned into the drive at about 3.15, it was dark and snowing. It looked like Dartmoor with all its buildings in a dark grey colour. How depressing the place looked.*
>
> (*At Loggerheads with the Enemy*, Bemrose 1981)

And another of a journey home and back by a patient on a long-awaited trip home:

> *John used to walk from the gates to Whitmore Station – a good eight miles – to catch the train to Stockport. He returned via Market Drayton, thence by Meredith's questionable bus service back to the lodge gates.*
>
> *(Ibid)*

Imagine such a journey undertaken on a regular basis to visit a relative! Imagine a young wife with two or three children trying to keep in touch with an invalid husband on the all-too-scanty visiting days. It would have been considered lunatic on her part even to try. In these circumstances TB must have seemed like, and sometimes was, a sentence of permanent separation.

Visitors were not, in any case, encouraged. Relapses after recovery were so common that patients were led to see their lives as permanently changed and to accept a lifestyle predicated on the sanatorium. Patients often stayed on site permanently as service or laboratory staff. Besides sparing sufferers the stress and hurly-burly of normal life, there would, as a result, be fewer sources of infection within the community.

Infection appeared to be a two-way exchange in some eyes; the superintendant of the sanatorium at Loggerheads was known to see his patients' visitors as an unmitigated nuisance because of the germs they imported into the sanatorium. In many sanatoria tales abounded of children brought to see a sick parent or sibling, who got no further than the fence marking the sanatorium boundary and would have been lucky to see the object of their visit as a miniaturised figure at a distance.

Sadly, the handicaps of a restricted existence were not limited to patients. Many doctors and nurses, in the nature of their work, developed TB, went into sanatoria as patients and made tuberculosis their specialism, staying to treat the patients there or in another chest hospital.

Sir Robert Philip was to make some changes to this scenario. So successful was the Edinburgh System in reducing deaths from TB that some years later, after reinforcement by the London Clinic, it was adopted as the most successful pattern of treatment for tuberculosis patients over the country. Its success was confirmed by the superintendent of the Paddington Clinic, where infections fell by 50% after adopting the Edinburgh System.

The hospital at Loggerheads, known as the Cheshire Joint because it served parts of Cheshire, Shropshire and Staffordshire, was one of the sanatoria built as a result of this change of direction. The new sanatoria were still, however, sited away from centres of dense population, since this was the cheaper option. Mortality figures over a wider area fell faster and further than before. Sir Robert felt able to predict that infection from the disease would be history within thirty years and looked like proving his boast.

But he was reckoning without the scourge of war. The Great War did not disturb the pattern to any great extent, but a government decision of sheer lunacy in World War II did.

In order to fulfil the perceived need for beds for war-wounded soldiers, sailors and airmen, as well as civilian casualties, 8,000 TB patients were decanted into the community, where infection spread like wildfire. At the worst of the TB epidemic in Victorian times, one in five of all deaths was from the disease. In 1943, after having substantially fallen in the years before the war, the figure was up again to one in seven and went on climbing for ten years after the war ended. (Sir Robert Philip had died in 1939 and was spared this heart-breaking reversal of his hopes.)

1950-51, the year of my hospitalization, was exactly halfway through this nerve-wracking, post-war decade of suspense. By its end control was re-established and, thanks to the magical effect of PAS, streptomycin and isoniazid, the number of deaths was falling again.

This triple cocktail of drugs as an efficient agent of recovery was inaugurated by Sir John Crofton after his appointment as Professor of Tuberculosis at Edinburgh University and, although new medicines have had to replace these as the bug became resistant to them, a triple or sometimes quadruple cocktail has remained the effective cure.

But the price of freedom is eternal vigilance. However successful the care programme, visitors from countries without such care are going to keep the problem alive and the more recent interloper, the HIV organism, has complicated matters by weakening the immune systems of its sufferers, so that they too are falling victim to TB (and, as newly discovered, leprosy.) In the present circumstances only a system as rigorous as the Edinburgh System of Sir Robert Philip, rolled out over the entire world, might possibly, sometime in the future, exterminate the TB bacillus.

Our mortality rate here in Britain is less than 1:100,000. In Canada, a civilised and forward-thinking country, it is

4:100,000. In the developing countries it can outstrip the nightmarish count of our worst years. In these countries there is neither education nor medicine nor funding to counter its ravages, but initiatives are not lacking. The battle is not yet won in the wider world, but the way ahead is clear.

APPENDIX
A Personal History of Tuberculosis Research and Treatment

By Professor Sir John Crofton

During the War I served in the Royal Army Medical Corps mostly in the Middle East. I diagnosed a number of tuberculosis patients but they were soon evacuated to South Africa. After demobilization in 1945 I was asked by the Medical Research Council TB Unit to coordinate the first classical controlled TB trial at Brompton Hospital (the major chest hospital in London.) The trial was also conducted in other UK centres. Patients all had advanced pulmonary tuberculosis.

Rest and good food was the only treatment given to the patients acting as controls in the trial. Controls would avoid any possible side-effects from streptomycin, but they would be entitled to treatment with streptomycin later if it proved effective.

Initially the streptomycin patients improved much more rapidly but, after 4-6 weeks, in many their bacilli then became drug-resistant. They often relapsed and died.

However, in 1948 a second drug, PAS, (para-amino salicylic acid) became available. The MRC carried out a second trial on three groups. They were allocated variously to streptomycin alone, PAS alone, or a group that were given both: PAS in cachets by the mouth, streptomycin by injection. The combined PAS/streptomycin group developed much less drug-resistance and had fewer deaths. Many recovered.

This was the state of play when I moved to Edinburgh in June 1952. Scotland and Edinburgh were in the middle of an extensive epidemic of TB. During the Second World War all

European countries had vast increases in TB, but Scotland and Portugal were the only European countries where there continued to be a sharp increase in new cases from year to year. The reasons for these increases were not known.

In Edinburgh I found myself in formal clinical charge of 400 TB beds in hospitals with another 400 on the waiting list for beds. But there was so much public concern that it was easy to persuade the Health Board to appoint two additional consultants and to move another from East and West Lothian to Edinburgh. Moreover, with the development of the NHS, the money in the Trust which had supported Sir Robert Philip's work was now available for our own research which it generously supported.

For the first two years our research concentrated on a detailed study of individual patients to find out why treatment often failed. We found that this was always due to drug-resistance, as patients on the waiting list had often, by present standards, received haphazard chemotherapy.

Moreover, we had two patients whom we found to have been primarily infected by bacilli already resistant to one of the pair of drugs given in treatment. Resistance tests took six weeks at that time. By the time we learnt about the primary resistance their bacilli had also become resistant to the second drug. We therefore decided it was safer to start off all new patients with all three drugs now available. Isoniazid had been introduced earlier in 1952.

To our astonishment we found we were curing all new patients. To our further astonishment, when we took over the whole clinical control in 1954 and ensured that all patients, including those on the waiting list, had all three drugs, the previously steadily increasing incidence of TB was reduced by 59% within three years and continued to fall steadily. But nobody in the UK, and few internationally, believed us. We were even accused of fiddling our figures.

By this time I was working with the International Union Against Tuberculosis (IUAT), of which Philip was one of the founders, and was chairman of their Chemotherapy Scientific Committee. My friend Noel Rist of the Pasteur Institute, one of the few who believed our results, was chairman of the Bacteriological Committee. He said to me, 'Look, John, they will never believe you until they see it in their own patients'.

So we organized a trial in 23 different countries. We chose one influential centre in each country in order to have a hoped-for ripple effect. All the patients had to be new and seriously ill. We dressed it up as *A Study of Causes of Failure in Far Advanced Pulmonary Tuberculosis.* But they all agreed to treat with a combination of all three drugs. As we were confident of a successful result, a control group would have been unethical.

I had worked in the Medical Reasearch Council (MRC) at Brompton Hospital with Reg Bignall. I thought he was a good organiser and good with people. He agreed to coordinate the trial. He also did not believe our previous figures so he would not be accused of fiddling them.

It all worked out as we hoped. Apart from one or two deaths in desperately ill patients in the early weeks, Reg found all the failures were where the local doctor changed the triple treatment. In general our claims were accepted. But once more it took 20 years, as with Philip, before virtually all centres in the UK were using good treatment.

Summary of other Scottish Research
(much via the Tuberculosis Society of Scotland)

1. In America patients treated with iso-nicotinic acid hydrazide (isoniazid or INH) had improved so rapidly it was thought that INH might be a metabolic stimulant. We did a double blind trial on ourselves and disproved this.

2. We persuaded our colleagues that, in mild non-infectious patients, bed rest might be unnecessary. So we did a controlled trial. Half of the patients had at least three months bed rest plus chemotherapy, the other half chemotherapy while living their normal lives, usually as bread-winners or family carers. The latter did just as well; bed rest was unnecessary.

3. Doubtfully active cases were usually watched regularly until they healed or became obviously active. We gave half of such patients different periods of preventive chemotherapy. We found it usually had to be more than six months to prevent most relapses.

4. American research had discovered that some patients metabolised INH quickly and claimed that the dose should be varied accordingly. In a carefully controlled trial we showed that this was unnecessary.

5. Corticosteroid drugs. Some workers had found that these sped up the cure, others that they resulted in deterioration. We suspected, and proved, that the bad results came from patients already with drug resistance. In patients with no drug resistance and good chemotherapy corticosteroids clinically improved them more rapidly and cleared their X-rays more rapidly but it

did not speed up the removal of tubercle bacilli from their sputa.

6. A junior colleague, Dr James Simpson, developed a test for PAS in the urine and showed that, in Out Patients, about 25% failed to take their drugs regularly. This proved to be a major problem worldwide.

7. Eighteen month treatment with current drugs proved necessary to prevent relapse in all cases however severe. This was confirmed by culture of surgically removed lungs after variable periods of chemotherapy and through a controlled trial by the MRC.

Other International Research
(Via the International Union Against Tuberculosis)

1. Drug Resistance Survey.
   a. Survey in 12 countries demonstrated a major problem both of primary and acquired resistance.
   b. Methods of testing proved very variable. (It was 30 years later that WHO carried out the next international survey and established standard test methods.)

2. Unreliability of X-ray diagnosis of TB via blind expert reading of a standard array of X-rays from Norwegian Mass Radiography.

3. Far greater reliability of sputum examination for bacilli (which the World Health Organisation (WHO) later adopted for the Directly Observed Treatment Shortcourse (DOTS) Programme.

The Third World 1963-1991

From 1963 to 1991 we had too few TB patients to carry out further research on TB in Scotland. I was very busy with successive University jobs as Dean of the Faculty of Medicine, Vice-Principal, writing a postgraduate book *Respiratory Diseases*, Presidency of the Royal College of Physicians and chairing a Scottish national committee to coordinate health education.

During this period, the British MRC turned its attention to the Third World. In association with the Indian MRC they showed that, with supervised chemotherapy, sanatorium treatment was unnecessary. Patients from the slums in Madras could be as well treated at home. They ceased to be infectious within two weeks. With the emergence of another powerful drug, rifampicin, they found, in East Africa, that the treatment period with combined drugs could be reduced from 18 to six or nine months.

A Czech refugee, Karel Styblo, working for the IUAT, also in East Africa, devised a simple, cheap treatment scheme. Patients could be diagnosed by sputum examination and treated by chemotherapy in routine health clinics and hospitals. Treatment could then be supervised and fully monitored till cured. This was the basis of the later WHO DOTS programme. The World Bank concluded that this was, in terms of years of life saved, the most cost-effective of any health measure, including infant vaccination. Accordingly the World Bank funded WHO to produce a global programme starting in 1992 with which I became involved.

The Edinburgh Group on Tuberculosis Control

The modern methods of TB Control were first developed in Edinburgh, building on research in chemotherapy by the Medical Research Council and our own research. This was very much a team effort. The following were important contributors:

Clinical Consultants: Dr Norman Horne. Special interest in non-pulmonary TB and special clinic for TB in pregnant women.

Dr Ian Ross. Special clinic for TB patients with diabetes or pneumoconiosis.

Dr Ian Grant. Special interest in non-TB chest disease.

Dr James Williamson (later Professor of Geriatrics). Special interest in running TB Dispensary and epidemiology.

Chief Bacteriologist: Dr Archie Wallace. Outstanding contributions on drug resistance.

Bacteriological Research Fellow: Sheila Stewart.

Clinical Research Fellows: Derek Turnbull, Ian Campbell and others.

Matron of Southfield Hospital: Miss Archibald.

Senior Social Worker: Miss Peggy Wood.

Chief Nurse at the Royal Victoria Dispensary: Miss Euphemia Liston.

Specialist TB Health Visitors: who supervised treatment at home and made sure relevant patient contacts were checked for TB.

Main Administrator: Alec Welstead. The best administrator I ever encountered in the NHS.

Medical Officer of Health: Dr Henry Seiler. Not a formal member of our team but someone with whom we worked closely, along with his colleagues.

Later Work for World Health Organisation

In 1991-2001, I chaired major WHO TB committees, including DOTS Recommendations and DOTS Plus (used for patients with drug resistance) and was extensively used as an advisor.

In 2001 I chaired a session of the joint WHO-World Bank meeting in Washington. I was asked to summarize achievements for the previous 50 years before Ministers of Health from most of the 22 high incidence countries, which joined with WHO and the World Bank to produce a plan to halve global TB in the next 15 years.

The HIV Pandemic
The incidence of TB in Tanzania was just beginning to fall when the HIV epidemic struck. That virus destroys the body's main cells which resist the tubercle bacillus. Patients become very susceptible to TB and are much more likely to be killed by the combined diseases. It has resulted in vast increases of TB in many countries.

The Future
The richer industrial countries now accept that HIV, tuberculosis and malaria are by far the most important major world threats to health. Much finance, though not yet enough, is becoming available internationally to provide drugs for treatment and to research for new drugs.

Drug resistance, due to misuse, is now also a major problem, which will need new drugs. The future, though a little more hopeful, is far from secure.